# the FOOL'S PILGRIMAGE

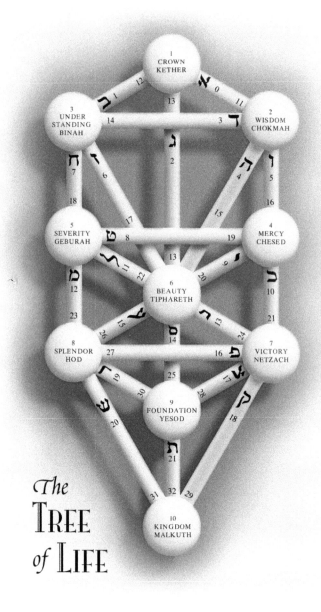

The
TREE
of LIFE

# *the* FOOL'S PILGRIMAGE

## Kabbalistic Meditations
### *on the* Tarot

STEPHAN A. HOELLER

Quest Books
Theosophical Publishing House
Wheaton, Illinois ◆ Chennai (Madras), India

*The Theosophical Society acknowledges with gratitude the generous support of the Kern Foundation for the publication of this book.*

Second Quest Edition 2004

The Theosophical Publishing House
P. O. Box 270
Wheaton, IL 60189-0270

·   Cover design, book design, and typesetting by Dan Doolin

Library of Congress Cataloging-in-Publication Data

Hoeller, Stephan A.
[Royal road]
The fool's pilgrimage: Kabbalistic meditations on the tarot / Stephan A. Hoeller.—
2nd Quest ed.
p.   cm.
Originally published: The royal road. Wheaton, Ill.: Theosophical Publishing House,
c1975.
ISBN 0-8356-0839-5
1. Tarot     2. Cabala      I. Title.

BF1879.T2H6 2004
133.3'2424—dc22

2003068979

5   4   3   2   1   *   04   05   06   07   08   09   10

*Printed in the United States of America*

*To the memory of*

*F. Israel Regardie*

# Contents

# PART II: PATH WORK ALONG THE ROYAL ROAD

# Preface to
## the Revised Edition

The collection of symbolic images that composes the Tarot deck has exercised a singular fascination on the minds and hearts of innumerable people over several centuries. Many have undoubtedly been attracted to the cards for their use in divination, known in its debased form as fortune-telling. The late "Hollywood Prophet" of television fame, Criswell, combined platitude with truth when he said: "We are all interested in the future, for that is where you and I will spend the rest of our lives!" In past ages, as well as using the Tarot, enthusiasts of divination frequently also resorted to casting the bones, divining by entrails, and deciphering the flight of birds—along with gazing into crystals and bowls of water. But today, it is mainly the Tarot, astrology, and the *I Ching* that are most usually employed for that purpose.

In addition to its ever-popular use as an instrument of divination, the Tarot deck also serves as a symbolic system of self-knowledge, self-integration, self-transformation, and self-transcendence. J. E. Cirlot, the noted authority on symbolism, writes regarding the work of depth psychologist C. G. Jung:

> Present-day psychology has confirmed . . . that the Tarot cards comprise an image (comparable to that encountered in dreams) of the path of initiation. At the same time Jung's view, coinciding with the secular, intuitive approach to the Tarot enigmas, recognized the portrayal of two different, but complimentary struggles in the life of man: (a) the struggle against others . . . and (b) [the struggle] against himself . . . involving individuation.*

* Juan-Eduardo Cirlot, *Dictionary of Symbols*, trans. Jack Sage (New York: Philosophical Library, 1962), 310.

The psychic resonance that the Tarot images tend to induce seems to be in no way diminished by rational considerations; and, indeed, the meaning of the Tarot is not discovered by discursive reasoning. Like all spiritually significant objects and practices, the Tarot poses a kind of riddle without apparent solution. It is thus that we are forced to rely on a certain *gnosis*—that is, our own inner knowing—in order to apprehend the meaning. We might use this insight for purposes either of our external lives (Jung's "the struggle against others") or of our spiritual growth ("the struggle with ourselves").

This book is devoted primarily to the way in which the twenty-two greater trump cards or Major Arcana of the Tarot serve as symbols for a particular method of meditation, the object of which is similar to what Jung calls "individuation," by which he means the life-long work of self-realization. In Kabbalistic language, the method is known as "path work." Meditation along the ways of the paths of the Kabbalistic Tree of Life is a practice that was first brought into public view by the fabled Order of the Golden Dawn, of which W. B. Yeats, S. L. MacGregor Mathers, W. W. Westcott, and A. E. Waite were some of the members. The late Dr. F. Israel Regardie, the last authentic representative of the original Golden Dawn tradition, frequently commented favorably on the earlier form of this book, and numerous readers have reported remarkable expansions of consciousness when using the twenty-two meditations it presents. Thus I feel justified when sending forth this revised and updated version, and I hope it will become a relevant and useful tool for explorers of consciousness in the twenty-first century.

Nearly thirty years have elapsed since the book's original publication, then entitled *The Royal Road*. Since that time, I have acquired modest fame as an interpreter of the Gnostic tradition to contemporary people. Accordingly, I need to address some questions that may be posed, such as: In what way do Tarot cards, with their various uses, relate to Gnosticism? Are they not part of the paraphernalia of the so-called New Age and hence unrelated to the lofty, transcendental concerns of Gnostics? The answer is simpler than expected: since gnosis has to do with intuitively perceived inner knowing, Gnostics welcome all means that stimulate such knowing—including the Tarot. Nor is divination per se foreign to Gnostic concerns. Throughout history, Gnostics have availed themselves of the synchronicities that occur in our earthly lives.

In conclusion, I wish to call attention to the audio CD included with this new edition. It is to be hoped that my reading of the meditation texts may simplify the practices recommended herein. Some might even welcome the voice they may have already heard in taped lectures or on the Gnostic website: <www.gnosis.org> In any case, I want to wish all of my readers "Bon voyage" on this pilgrimage!

—Stephan A. Hoeller
*April 2004*

# PREFACE *to* *the* ORIGINAL EDITION

During the years 1972 and 1973, the task devolved upon me to conduct several classes throughout Southern California dealing with the combined use of the Tarot cards and the symbolic philosophy of the Kabbalah. In the course of these sessions, I was impelled to compose twenty-two brief meditations, expressing the quintessence of what I conceived to be the principal spiritual experiences embodied in each of the twenty-two paths connecting the ten sephiroth on the Tree of Life, with special reference to the symbolic representations of the paths in the twenty-two cards of the Tarot Major Arcana.

As my work developed, interest grew both in the subject in general and in the texts of the meditations in particular. Numerous students came to regard the meditations as very helpful to their endeavors in the direction of experiencing the qualities of the paths and Tarot Arcana. Increasingly, the suggestion was brought forward that I make these meditation texts available to a larger public. It was suggested that I also present, at least in outline form, the philosophical and mystical rationale behind the practice of meditating with the aid of the Tarot and the Kabbalah. Flowing naturally from these various considerations, there emerged the present work, which is chiefly intended to serve as a handbook of Kabbalistic meditation on the Major Arcana of the Tarot; however, depending on the readers' inclination, it may serve other, ancillary purposes as well. Since this treatise does not presuppose any previous background of reading and study within the fields of either the Kabbalah or the Tarot, it may be considered a primer of these subjects, in addition to being a guide to a specific practice of meditation. It is thus my hope that my efforts will furnish an appropriate introduction to a topic that is essentially inexhaustible and a veritable fountainhead of unending delights and wonders.

The system of meditation and of the mystical philosophy outlined in this small work is a symbolic one. Symbolic systems exist in order to make available to the aspirant the ciphers of the mystery. They are designed to place into the hands of the student a set of keys whereby the portals of the secret chambers may be unlocked. Whether and how the person desirous of the inner light may make use of the cipher, and in what manner he will apply the keys, is his own individual task, in which no teacher or author can assist him past a certain point. Like Moses of old, the symbols can only lead us to the very boundary of the Promised Land, where another leader, in this case our own desire for truth and light, must complete the task of the great conquest. This journey, sometimes called the Royal Road, must be trod by the reader himself: the present manual can at best serve only as an inducement, a hint, a finger pointing at the moon. Earthly books are pale reflections of the Book of Life, and all words are but inadequate substitutes for the Lost Word which must be found within ourselves. The Royal Road, which in ancient China was also called *Tao*, "the way," has most aptly been characterized by Lao-tse, when he said:

> *The way that can be told*
> *Is not the constant way;*
> *The name that can be named*
> *Is not the eternal name.*

—Stephan A. Hoeller
*January 1975*

# NOTE *to the* READER

T he cards of the Tarot Major Arcana used as illustrations in this work are those designed by the renowned occult and magic scholar A. E. Waite, and executed by the artist, Pamela Colman Smith. In the present, revised edition, extensive use has been made of the Universal Waite Tarot Deck, with new coloring by Mary Hanson-Roberts, conceived by Stuart R. Kaplan, but containing the original designs of the Waite, or Rider pack. These cards have the additional advantage of having been designed with the specific objective in mind of embodying the Kabbalistic symbology related to the Tree of Life. The only major difference between this deck and some older packs is that Strength is the VIII-th Arcanum (earlier number XI) and Justice is the XI-th Arcanum (earlier number VIII). The attributions of the Arcana to the paths of the Tree of Life are those of the Golden Dawn system, adhered to by most modern authorities, including A. E. Waite and Paul Foster Case.

He who has to start on a journey very early should rise at day-break and look carefully toward the east. Then he will perceive certain signs resembling letters that pierce through the sky and appear above the horizon. These shining forms are those of the letters wherewith God created heaven and earth.                —The Zohar

The Tarot is a truly philosophical machine, which keeps the mind from wandering, while leaving its initiative at liberty; it is mathematics applied to the Absolute, the alliance of the positive and the ideal, a lottery of thoughts as exact as numbers, perhaps the simplest and grandest conception of human genius. . . . An imprisoned person, with no other book than the Tarot, if he knew how to use it, could in a few years acquire universal knowledge and would be able to speak on all subjects with unequalled learning and inexhaustible eloquence.                —Eliphas Levi

# Acknowledgments

Grateful appreciation is extended to the many people who assisted in the completion of this volume, especially:

the late *Forest E. Barber*—
    for his tireless efforts in correcting the manuscript

*Bryan Campbell*—
    for giving me devoted and expert assistance over the years; and in this instance, for his work with recording the reading of the meditations on the CD accompanying this book

*Michael V. N. Leavitt*—
    for offering invaluable advice on the Kabbalah, into the mysteries of which he introduced many, including the author

# INTRODUCTION

As even the most casual observer is likely to note, the twenty-two picture cards of the Tarot Major Arcana possess an imagery of a unique psychological power that is strangely evocative of unexpected intuitions and glimpses of a world beyond the senses. Many a person upon purchasing a deck of Tarot cards has found himself unexplainably drawn to these pictures; and, after allowing their imagery to penetrate his consciousness, has experienced a veritable flooding of his mind and emotions by insights, feelings, and concepts of an unusual and fascinating character. Those who subsequently have availed themselves of one of the now quite numerous popular treatises on the Tarot have then learned that these twenty-two Trump cards have a certain relationship to the mysterious and venerable system of mystical lore known as the Kabbalah, and that the cards derive much of their symbolic meaning and evocative qualities from their position within the grand Kabbalistic design known as the Tree of Life.

The mysteries of the Kabbalah, much more than those of the Tarot, have been held in awe and reverence by large numbers of people over a very long period of time. The authoritative literature dealing with the Kabbalah has, until quite recently, been at once too abstruse, too technical, and too expensive for the ordinary reader; consequently, some students of the occult have tended to shy away from it altogether. In addition to these very practical obstacles to the study of the Kabbalah, there were and are numerous other reasons for the reluctance of many to become involved in its lore. More than any other system of mysticism, the Kabbalah appears to release with extreme speed and power various psychological forces from the unconscious of its students, and this fact has earned it a not entirely undeserved reputation of being somewhat hazardous. Further, considering the undisputable fact that numerous practitioners of magic, many of doubtful intentions and eccentric behavior, have attempted to utilize Kabballistic teachings for their purposes, it is easy to comprehend why many well-intentioned people, fearful of becoming involved with sorcery, have devoted their efforts to other, presumably less tainted, disciplines of mysticism.

During the last three decades of the twentieth century, the Western world experienced a phenomenal interest in all things mystical, magical, and occult. One of the fortunate by-products of this tidal wave has been the diminishing of apprehension on the part of students concerning the so-called dangers of practical occultism and applied mysticism. Perhaps in an era of world wars, hydrogen bombs, the increasingly real hazards of pollution, and all the additional facts bearing witness to the inhumanity of the age of science and reason, it has become easier for intelligent people of all ages to retreat from scientific rationalism and, in the course of this retreat, to be less fearful of magic with its often misunderstood but much publicized horrors. Indeed, the attitude toward magic has undergone a considerable liberalization; the more sensational practitioners are now generally regarded as no more than harmless enthusiasts or, at worst, flamboyant dabblers. While it is not our intention to debate the merits and dangers of the occult arts, there is certainly no reason in these days for shunning the Kabbalah as some sort of an occult plague.

Among people possessing a good measure of Kabbalistic learning, one frequently encounters those who seem rather to relish the abstruseness and so-called esotericism of the relevant literature; they continue to point out that the Kabbalah was and is not for the masses and should be reserved for the select few. In the ranks of these esotericists, we find both pious Jews and non-Jewish Kabbalists, all of whom are in accord when assuming that much prior training of character, intellect, and spirit are necessary before a student can profit from the Kabbalistic system. Whatever the merits of this attitude might have been in the past, their justification is small indeed now. Who would propose in all seriousness at present that before a man (and certainly a woman!) could study the Kabbalah, he ought to be married, forty years old, and have a full stomach? Such injunctions were perhaps suitable to the life-style of

2

a seventeenth-century ghetto, but they are certainly unfitted to the conditions of the dweller in the megalopolis of twenty-first-century America or Europe. Not that the contention of the need for a certain level of readiness in such studies and practices is in itself without foundation! Far from it. Fools and knaves have ever found their ways into the sacred precincts of the mysteries, and many an initiate found himself impelled to drive them out, not unlike Jesus is reported to have done with the moneychangers in the temple.

Upon deeper reflection, one finds little if any reason for the kind of esotericism that engages in a deliberate obscuration and concealment of mystical knowledge. A system of authentic mysticism inevitably possesses its own ready-made defenses against any real intrusion into its mysteries by the unqualified or the malicious. These defenses or safeguards are all grounded in the absolutely basic tendency of every authentic system of the mysteries toward the diminishing of the human ego and the consequent increase of a Higher Self, which is totally impersonal, altruistic, and universally beneficent in nature and in activity. Thus we need not fear that the selfish, the greedy, and those hungering for satisfaction of the myriad desires of the human ego will gain additional power for the attainment of their objectives from the Kabbalah. If perchance they should as much as venture into the outer court of the temple of the mysteries of the Tree of Life, the limitations of their own personalities would compel them to withdraw in haste and disappointment. To the hoary admonition not to cast pearls before swine, we might answer that, given a choice, swine have always preferred a diet of corn to one of pearls! No one the least bit informed concerning the profusion of allegedly spiritual and occult systems could deny that today the choice is indeed great, and thus the metaphysical porcine will have little difficulty in locating the kind of feed appropriate to his tastes.

The Kabbalah is not only for the learned and the pious; it is for all of us. Like most other systems of genuine mysticism, it is like the ocean, wherein a small child can cool his feet in the shallows, while at the same time a deep-sea diver may penetrate to many fathoms in search of sunken treasure. It is no doubt true that in olden days the learned Rabbis, who guarded the Kabbalah as the most precious gem of their faith, insisted that only one proficient in the Torah, or Law, might be found worthy to touch the Kabbalah. It may be useful to realize that the divine law must, of necessity, be universal in character. Devotees of any faith, or of none, may master it and live in accordance with its precepts, thereby acquiring the qualifications of a Kabbalist. Learning of itself seldom leads to wisdom, which is an essential of the inward quest of the mystic. Similarly, conventional religiosity, with its frequent reliance on blind faith and rigid moral codes, cannot be properly regarded as the right preparatory training for the pursuit of mysticism. More often than not, such religious belief and practice becomes an end in itself instead of leading its devotee to a position of deeper insight and superior wisdom, not to speak of mystic union with the Divine Power.

There are other reasons why the Kabbalah should be considered uniquely suited to the needs, not only of the determined seeker after divine illumination, but also of the busy man and woman of the work-a-day world, as also of the occultist, mildly intrigued by true mystical pursuits. Many of the subjects with which metaphysical and occult studies bring us in contact are so far removed from the experiences and interests of everyday life that preoccupation with them leads the aspirant farther and farther away from the practical and legitimate concerns of living. While one feels drawn towards such occult theories by an attraction that increases in geometrical progression with the increase in knowledge, one remains yet conscious of a sense of unreality, or at least impracticality, while dealing with them. When, in so many books of this sort, one reads of the formation of the solar system, of the rounds and chains of planets and galaxies ensouled by Logoi and populated by diverse races of souls, or when one becomes immersed in accounts of mysterious master adepts directing the course of the world from the Himalayas or the Gobi Desert, one cannot but feel that, fascinating though such statements are as abstract studies or exercises in fantasy, they nevertheless associate themselves at best only indirectly with the life we are living at present.

No such objection, however, can be taken to our present subject: the system of the Kabbalah, as practically manifest in the Tarot Major Arcana. This system, especially when understood and practiced as a discipline of inward realization, is of the greatest and most evident usefulness and practicality imaginable. The universal glyph of the Tree of Life is a symbol of such general applicability that every conceivable fact, idea, and activity of life can readily be related to it and thus receive a degree of illumined meaning not ordinarily accessible to human thought. In addition, the Tree of Life, as illustrated by the Tarot Arcana, permits the individual consciousness to partake of a series of spiritual experiences, all so ordered on the basis of a superbly designed plan that they will gradually lead the soul from superficiality to profundity, from confusion to understanding; nay, even from humanity to divinity. It is not our intention here to discuss the justification for combining the two outwardly independent disciplines of the Kabbalah and the Tarot for the purpose of the expansion and deepening of soul awareness by way of meditation: this subject we shall mention in the course of the main text. Nevertheless, some general remarks might be in order:

One of the many explanations for the mysterious word *Tarot* is that it is taken from Egyptian words *Tar*, meaning "Path," and *Ro*, *Ros*, and *Rog*, together meaning "The Royal Path of Life" or "The Royal Road." Legend tells us that some time after the destruction of the mysteries of antiquity and prior to the onset of the Dark Ages, certain wise men gathered in Fez, in Morocco, and there designed or constructed what might be called a textbook in pictures, wherein they concentrated in symbolic form the occult teachings and mystical experiences that served as the inner content of the mysteries. It is more likely than not that this legend has little if any basis in fact. Nevertheless, it tells an important story. A picture is worth many thousands of words; and if the picture corresponds to the archetypal and primordial images resident within the unconscious of man, the study and contemplation of such a picture can indeed give rise to great transforming experiences within the psyche. This being in fact the case with the Tarot Arcana, it is obvious why, at all times, they have held so many people bound in their spell of wonder and mystery. The Kabbalah, with its great symbolic diagram of the Tree of Life, serves a similar, although more all-encompassing, purpose. Need we be amazed, therefore, that these two disciplines, Tarot and Kabbalah, have been combined to accomplish, or at least advance, the purpose to which they are both dedicated?

The Tarot and Kabbalah serve two main purposes. First, they preserve and transmit an esoteric philosophy, a teaching of a special nature. Second, they both evoke specific conscious and unconscious responses from the psyche of the student who has learned how to observe and meditate upon the symbols involved. It is this second common objective that has led to the combined use of Tarot and Kabbalah when employed for the purpose of meditation.

In the following pages, we are chiefly concerned with what in Kabbalistic terminology is called "path work," or the travel of the individual consciousness upward on the Tree of Life, thus deepening its own contact with its true roots in divinity, or the world of the psychological archetypes, to use the terminology of C. G. Jung. The paths, twenty-two in number, are symbolized by the twenty-two picture cards of the Major Arcana, which can serve as illustrations or pictorial representations of the spiritual experiences represented by the paths. By meditating on the proper Tarot Arcanum, we thus may invoke into our personality, or bring into our conscious awareness, the experience represented by it, which in turn is analogous to the experience of the particular path on the Tree of Life. Since the purpose of the present manual is to aid the aspirant in his meditations on the cards and in experiencing the deeper realities attendant on such meditations, all descriptions of the Tree of Life, or of the Tarot deck, not directly related to this purpose have been omitted. For this reason, the ten sephiroth are described only briefly, but the paths connecting the sephiroth are treated in greater detail. Many other teachings connected with the Tree of Life, such as the Four Worlds, the Lightning Flash, the Abyss, the Kliphoth, and many others, are either not mentioned at all or referred to only within the context of the meditations on the spiritual experiences of the paths. While these omissions would be inexcusable in any work, no matter how elementary, purporting to deal with either the Tarot or the Kabbalah, it is the conviction of the writer that in a short handbook of Kabbalistic meditation on the Tarot Arcana most of the omitted material would have been confusing to the novice and, at the same time, redundant to the seasoned Kabbalist and Tarot student.

Perhaps among those who in this small book catch their first glimpse of the grandeur of the Kabbalah, there may be a few who will be led to penetrate more deeply into its philosophy, cosmology, psychology, and mysticism, facing its more abstruse problems with the student's zeal and the neophyte's ardor. Perchance it may even happen that some already learned in the profound secrets of the Kabbalah and well acquainted with the fascinating world of the Tarot will find some inspiration or stimulation within the pages that follow. Above all, however, one may hope that people in all walks of life and of every age group, religious persuasion, and philosophical orientation, possessing a degree of eagerness wherewith they can approach the fathomless mystery of their own inner being, might be substantially aided by the practice of guided meditation that the writer here presents. Until comparatively recently, occult and spiritual movements, as well as individual students, suffered greatly because of the lack of practical work within their chosen field of interest. Happily a new aeon, the Aquarian Age, is upon us, wherein active occultism, operative magic, and practical mysticism are replacing the textbook version of the mysteries that enthralled nineteenth- and early twentieth-century seekers. Occultism is changing in character, acquiring a quality of openness. Occult means hidden, and all things hidden can become plain and open to they who travel the Royal Road to the palace and temple of the kingly wisdom of the soul. May this handbook aid many while on that pilgrimage!

## PART I

PREPARING
FOR THE
JOURNEY

# The WISDOM of
# the TAROT

T he true origin of the images of the Tarot is shrouded in a
seemingly impenetrable mystery. One of the earliest accounts
dates back to ancient Egypt, where, according to legend, on
the altar of the temple of Ptah in Memphis images were found
engraved on plates of gold, which resembled certain of the greater
Trumps, or Major Arcana, of the Tarot. The French scholar, Court
de Gebélin, writing in his noted work, *Le Monde Primitif*, in 1781,
asserted that the Tarot is, in fact, the one book of the ancient
Egyptians that escaped the burning of the Alexandrian Library and
that, moreover, it contains "the purest knowledge of profound matters" possessed by the wise men of Egypt. Numerous more recent
students of the Tarot tend to regard the above account as an exag-
geration and humbly confess their ignorance of the origins of the
cards. Nevertheless, the Egyptian hypothesis has numerous illustrious followers, including Eliphas Levi, Paul Christian, Papus, and
others. In the view of many, the Tarot originated in the mysterious,
long-lost Book of Thoth, attributed to the god of secret wisdom,
Thoth, better known under his Greek name of Hermes.

By the fourteenth century, Tarot images had reached Spain,
Italy, and France and were transported to other countries by the
Romany, or "Gypsy," people, who appear to have used the images
mainly for purposes of fortune-telling. There are shadowy indications, however, to the effect that images resembling the Tarot were
circulating in various forms long before the fourteenth century.

While historical inquiry into the origins of the Tarot leads us
at best to the Gypsy caravans and, at worst, nowhere, the area of

myth and legend yields far more promising results. It has been rightly said that myth is of greater authenticity than history because it deals with the timeless realities of the soul, instead of with the pale reflections of these realities on the illusory screen of time and fact. Thus we find that the myth of the origins of the Tarot is, indeed, far more revealing than its history. Mystical tradition tells us that after the final destruction of the great library of Alexandria and at the beginning of the Dark Ages, certain wise men who met in the city of Fez, Morocco, decided to create a medium whereby the initiatory wisdom of antiquity might be preserved for future generations. In their prophetic foresight, these sages knew that the tyrannical medieval Church would destroy any such device if it were apparent that it contained ideas and symbols inimical to what was regarded as Christian orthodoxy. These sages also knew that illiteracy would be the order of the day for many centuries and that, therefore, a verbal and written transmission of the wisdom would be useless. The old adepts, so the legend tells us, then decided to construct *a picture book* of universal knowledge that would escape the attention of the inquisitors and continue for countless years to remind men and women of the deeper truths of life and of the essential character of their own being.

If, indeed, this tale has any basis in fact, it indicates the profound psychological knowledge of the sages in question. A picture is worth many thousands of words, and if the picture corresponds to the archetypal or primordial images resident within the unconscious of humankind, the study and contemplation of such a picture can give rise to outstanding transforming experiences within the psyche. Depth psychologist C. G. Jung aptly stated that "He who speaks in primordial images speaks to us as with a thousand trumpets, he grips and overpowers, and at the same time he elevates that which he treats out of the individual and transitory into the sphere of the eternal."[*] If the Tarot cards are, indeed, the product of a consciously designed effort on the part of some unknown individuals designed to stimulate the powers resident in the primordial images

[*] Jolande Jacobi, ed., *Psychological Reflections* (New York: Harper Torchbooks, 1961), 181.

of the unconscious, these author-artists would have to be gratefully and reverently congratulated. If, on the other hand, the Tarot was not devised but evolved according to some mysterious inner plan of its own, this possibility would only deepen the mystery and make our hearts beat even faster when approaching it. Whether the small acorn of a deck of cards was planted ages ago by spiritual giants, or whether it fell fortuitously from an unknown height into the soil of the psyche of Western civilization, it has grown into a mighty, sacred oak tree, giving shade, comfort, and delight to countless men and women for generations without number. Like a tree, the Tarot lives and grows; rooted in earth, nourished by water, warmed by the solar fire, it reaches with its crown into the airy space of limitless eternity. As an instrument of cognition, it has almost no equal; the knowledge gained by its study extends from cosmology and cosmogony, through philosophy, astrology, alchemy, and magic to psychological analysis and self-knowledge. Wherever and whatever its beginnings, in a very real sense it is still for us the Book of Thoth, a scroll of pictures brought from the high heavens of wisdom by Hermes, messenger of gods and teacher of men.

The wise alone know how to employ vice as well as virtue in order to advance the cause of good. On the surface, wisdom and gambling have little in common; they are antithetical in nature. Still, had it not been for the vice of gambling, the compendium of wisdom known as the Tarot might have been lost. The cards, which probably originally were made of leather or metal, were used as a means of gambling and amusement and thus were cherished by many who did not value philosophy or mysticism. The Tarot cards became playing cards. The mysterious images were unknowingly used by the ignorant and the frivolous as a means of transmitting the wisdom of the ages.

The complete deck of the Tarot consists of seventy-eight individual cards, which are divided into two groups: the fifty-six cards of the so-called Minor Arcana and the twenty-two cards of the Major Arcana, the latter also being known as the Greater Trumps. The fifty-six cards of the Minor Arcana are the origin of our modern playing cards. They are divided into four suits—namely,

Pentacles, Cups, Swords, and Wands—each of which consists of ten cards numbered one through ten and four court cards, which are King, Queen, Knight, and Page. The Major Arcana consists of twenty-two keys or trumps numbered zero through twenty-one.

Opinions differ as to which of the Tarot suits gave rise to which modern playing card suit, but the most likely classification runs as follows:

> *Pentacles*, indicating interest, money: *Diamonds*
>
> *Cups*, indicating love, happiness: *Hearts*
>
> *Swords*, indicating strife, misfortune: *Spades*
>
> *Wands*, indicating glory, enterprise: *Clubs*

In the course of time, the gambling inventiveness of mankind simplified the Tarot and reduced it to various more limited decks, consisting variously of fifty-four, thirty-two, and even twenty-four cards, which are used for such games as Whist, Bridge, Skat, Poker, Remy, Piquet, and others. The twenty-two cards of the Major Arcana were totally eliminated from most decks of playing cards, with the exception of the Joker, a corrupted form of the Fool of the Major Arcana. Trump cards closely resembling the Greater Trumps of the Tarot can be found, however, in a deck of playing cards popular in Central Europe, called *Tarock*.

Hand in hand with the increased use of the Minor Arcana of the Tarot for gaming purposes went the neglect of these same fifty-six suit cards by occult students, who, beginning with Eliphas Levi in the nineteenth century, began to concentrate their attention almost exclusively on the twenty-two symbolic cards of the Major Arcana. The present writer regards this tendency as an understandable but unfortunate error. The universe and the human being (who is a universe in miniature) consist of two major dimensions. The first of these is the outer, or lesser, dimension, consisting of the aspect of things as revealed to us by our senses, as reacted to by our feelings, as evaluated by our intellect, and as apprehended by our intuition. As against this outer, comprehensible, operative world, we can also recognize the existence of another, far more mysterious, but infinitely richer sphere of being, which in terms of Jungian psychology we might name the abode of the archetypes of the collective unconscious. The first or outer realm is the one depicted by the fifty-six cards of the Minor Arcana, while the second or inner realm is indicated by the twenty-two symbolic cards of the Major Arcana. Together, they make up a complete, unobstructed, and undivided symbolic representation of macrocosmic and microcosmic reality. The attempt on the part of some occultists and mystics to ignore the fifty-six suit cards is for the most part indicative of their predilection to withdraw into the mysterious inner world of their secret selves and, at the same time, neglect the visible, intelligible side of the outer world and of their personal cosmos. It is our intention to show the nature and relationship of these two areas of existence as demonstrated to us by the Tarot.

As a general rule, we can say that the fifty-six cards of the Minor Arcana represent the outer self or *personality* of man, while the twenty-two cards of the Major Arcana symbolize the secret kingdom of the inner self or *individuality*. The two follow separate but related laws of operation, as symbolized in the Tarot in several ways, of which the system of numbers may be mentioned here as a particularly interesting example. The Minor Arcana are constructed on the basis of the numbers four and ten, since there are four suits, with ten numbered cards and four court cards to each. The Major Arcana are based on the numbers three and seven, inasmuch as the twenty-two cards can most usefully be divided into three septenaries plus the zero card, which defies classification, or $3 \times 7 = 21 + 0$. It may also be noted that each suit of the Minor Arcana has fourteen cards, and that fourteen is the number given by H. P. Blavatsky in *The Secret Doctrine* as the totality of manifestation: "The twice seven, the sum total." On the other hand, the numbers three and seven when added instead of multiplied give us the number ten, which is the number of the sephiroth on the Kabbalistic Tree of Life. This might be taken to indicate that the principle of the numbers three and seven as manifest in the Major

Arcana describes the structure of the god-powers in things, while the principle of the numbers four and ten as present in the Minor Arcana symbolizes the natural, or created, aspect of being; the former relates to life, while the latter indicates form.

Since the primary objective of the Tarot appears to be the facilitation of self-knowledge, it is necessary for us to look at the cards primarily in terms of their correspondences with psychological functions and principles within the human psyche. Thus the ten numbered cards and the four court cards of the four suits of the Minor Arcana together correspond to the four basic functions of consciousness as described by Jung; namely, sensation, feeling, thinking, and intuition. At the same time, we must keep in mind that the twenty-two symbolic cards of the Major Arcana are representatives of the primordial images, or archetypes, within the collective unconscious.

One of the most ancient, and also most useful, symbolic representations of the human personality is the circle, intersected by an equal-armed cross. This is the design used also for the Zodiac and for the yearly calendar, divided into the four seasons by the equinoxes and solstices, which, when connected by straight lines, form the cross within the circle. The alchemists and magicians of old employed this fourfold classification of being when speaking of the four magical "elements" of Earth, Water, Fire, and Air and when referring to the four alchemical substances of Mercury, Sulphur, Salt, and Water. This perennially recurring quaternary structure was also employed by Jung in his classification of psychological types and, even more importantly, of the functions of human consciousness.

In Jungian terms, it takes little imagination to recognize that the ancient "element" of earth, when psychologically understood, is analogous to the function of sensation, as water stands for emotion, fire for thinking, and air for intuition. The analogy can further be extended to include the four suits of the Tarot, thus correlating the suit of Pentacles with the function of sensation, Cups with feeling, Swords with thinking, and Wands with intuition. Similarly, the four court cards of each suit may in turn be equated with the aforementioned psychological functions. Thus we may consider the following analogies:

| TAROT SUIT | FUNCTION | ELEMENT | ALCHEMY | COURT CARD |
|---|---|---|---|---|
| *Pentacles* | Sensation | Earth | Salt | *Page* |
| *Cups* | Feeling | Water | Water | *Queen* |
| *Swords* | Thinking | Fire | Sulphur | *Knight* |
| *Wands* | Intuition | Air | Mercury | *King* |

It is only fair to point out that when it comes to the attribution of the four ancient elements to the four suits of the Tarot, the authorities are in frequent disagreement with each other. Papus and Case make the suit of Wands correspond to Fire and Cups to Water, but Case connects Pentacles with Earth and Swords with Air, while Papus relates Swords to Earth and Pentacles to Air. The disagreement existing between these two eminent authorities may be taken as an example of the differences among Tarot students regarding attributions. It is almost universally recognized, however, that irrespective of whether it is related to Air or to Fire, the suit of Wands embodies a more subtle—and therefore more benign as well as more visionary—function of consciousness than does the suit of Swords. It is also almost beyond dispute that the suit of Pentacles relates to physical life and to material concerns, as against the emotional characteristics of the suit of Cups. With Pentacles, we are dealing with matters relating to perception through the senses; with Cups, we are involved in the weighing and reactive function of feeling; with Swords, we find ourselves in the realm of analysis through thinking; and with Wands, we move in the world of intuition, which is the inward apprehension of things in their totality. The usefulness of a system of attributions utilizing the four Jungian functions of consciousness to describe the qualities of the four suits of the Tarot is thus considerable indeed.

If we visualize the four suits of the Minor Arcana as the four sections of a circle, we might in turn envision the twenty-two symbolic Trump cards of the Major Arcana as links connecting the center of the circle with its periphery, not unlike the spokes connecting the rim of a wheel with its hub. The wheel is more than a fortuitous image when used in connection with the Tarot. Numerous students feel that the word *Tarot* represents an anagram of the Latin word for "wheel," *rota*. Using this analogy, we could liken the hub of the wheel to the zero card (the Fool) of the Major Arcana and the remaining twenty-one Trump cards to spokes, or portions of spokes of the wheel. The cards of the Major Arcana are, in fact, the carriers or transporters of the primordial psychic energy, proceeding from the center of our being to its periphery, where it becomes diffused and is allowed to circulate freely among the four functions. They symbolize psychological potencies that carry impressions from the outside of our personality into the unconscious, and conversely, conduct modifications of the inward power of the collective unconscious to the conscious level of our being. Thus the totality of selfhood, being a circle with its center everywhere and circumference nowhere, is represented to us by the structure of the great wheel, or rota, also known as the Tarot.

As stated previously, the Major Arcana consist of twenty-two cards numbered one through twenty-one and, in addition, having a most mysterious twenty-second card, a card without number, possessing the potency of zero and with the name of the "Fool." This card has been the cause of much disagreement among students of the Tarot. Some have placed it at the very end of the series of twenty-two, while others have inserted it between the twentieth and twenty-first cards. A seemingly much more logical position was assigned to the Fool by the Tarot scholars of the once-illustrious Hermetic Order of the Golden Dawn, who placed this card at the very beginning of the series of twenty-two, giving expression to the undeniable mathematical fact that zero comes before one.

The Fool or zero card is in many ways the most significant and most powerful of the cards of the Major Arcana, because it symbolizes the pristine spiritual source and ultimate destiny of all manifest powers and beings. It stands for the Alpha and Omega of manifestation, the No-Thing out of which all things proceed and into which they resolve at the end of the aeons. Being the symbol of this primal causeless cause, and thus utterly abstract and unsubstantial in nature, this card would spell foolishness to the worldly. From the vantage point of the spirit, all earthly gain is of no account; the road to earthly attainment leads nowhere, means nothing, and ends in nothing. The wisdom of the world is foolishness in the sight of the gods, and, conversely, the Divine Wisdom appears as foolishness in the sight of men, who, having become forgetful of their own divine heritage, have become *mere* men, instead of sons of the gods. It is quite easy to comprehend why to the uninitiated the Fool, or original spiritual potency, would appear as the embodiment of uselessness, silliness, and stupidity. All appearance is deception, and only at the center of the great circular dance of creation, where the Fool stands in still, motionless serenity, do we find that which no longer deceives by appearances, because it no longer appears, but is. Charles Williams, in his delightful occult novel *The Greater Trumps*, most insightfully describes the figures of the Tarot deck as performing an everlasting circular dance of great intricacy, within which the Fool occupies the motionless position of the pivot around which the entire dance revolves.

From the mysterious point of original and final unity, symbolized by the zero card, or the Fool, there proceed three streams, or spokes, each consisting of seven cards of the Major Arcana, together adding up to twenty-one. The first of these (one through seven, or from Magician to Chariot) stands for the area of creative powers, or of causes within the collective unconscious. The second septenary (eight through fourteen, or Strength through Temperance) consists of representations of the laws by which the primordial powers of the first septenary are channeled toward manifestation. Third, the last septenary (fifteen through twenty-one, or Devil through World) symbolizes the results or finalized concrete manifestations of the first seven powers, as they appear in their actualized or differentiated condition.

CHAPTER TWO

# The ART of DIVINATION

A s we shall discuss in a further chapter, due to the close association of the Tarot with the Kabbalah, cards of the Major Arcana are attributed to each of the letters of the Hebrew alphabet, which leads in turn to the symbolic attribution of one card each to the paths, or channels, on the Kabbalistic Tree of Life. In addition, further analogies have been established between alchemical concepts and zodiacal and planetary symbols and the cards of the Major Arcana. The student should keep in mind, however, that the significance of the cards does not lie exclusively in their attribution to or correlation with other systems of symbolic philosophy. The Kabbalah, astrology, alchemy, and other occult disciplines shed a measure of additional light on the Tarot, but it must be clearly recognized that the *cards themselves* can be said to radiate their own special, and by no means negligible, light. The Tarot works as a means of cognition, whether or not we are able to relate it meaningfully to other systems. The cards speak directly to our intuition, to the unconscious potencies of our soul. He who becomes discouraged with the study of the Tarot on account of the differences of opinion existing among writers and teachers regarding attributions of elements, planets, zodiacal signs, letters of the Hebrew alphabet, and so forth has come to judge the precious jewel by the frequently inappropriate setting into which inept hands have placed it. Let the student be assured: the cards do not merely carry the reflected power of other occult arts, but possess and convey a mighty power of their very own.

Today, as ever, the Tarot owes its greatest measure of popularity to its use as a device for divination. Divination is not mere fortune-telling or superstition. Rather, it is an exceedingly subtle psychological technique whereby the secrets of the unconscious can be discovered, its powers (extrasensory and others) can be made accessible, and guidance for our confused and disordered lives can be obtained. The Tarot cards are one of the most ancient and most potent means of divination, second perhaps only to the Chinese *I Ching*, over which they possess the advantage of having closer affinity to the collective unconscious of Western culture. The exact nature of the psychology of successful divination is still a matter of conjecture, although modern depth psychology, especially through the theory of synchronicity advanced by C. G. Jung, has shed much light upon it.

The most important fact to fix in one's mind is that there is nothing haphazard or accidental in the universe, and that external events—no matter how seemingly trivial—are intimately related to happenings within the human psyche. Thus, if we learn the art of discovering and interpreting the external signs, we may thereby gain access to the world of inward realities in our own souls and in the soul of the cosmos. *The magic of Tarot divination is not in the cards but in ourselves.* The cards can and do act as instrumentalities whereby the subjective reality within the unconscious becomes able to project a portion of itself into objective existence. Through this projection, a meaningful and useful relationship or a creative dialogue between the subjective and objective sides of our lives may be established, which is a great accomplishment. Thus divination by means of the Tarot may be defined as a practical way in which a bridge is built between the temporal world of physical events, on the one hand, and the timeless world of the archetypes of the collective unconscious, on the other. It may be useful to recall that divination was considered an important part of the curriculum of certain mystery schools, not primarily in order to teach how to foretell the future, but in order to construct a psychic mechanism within the initiate whereby a source of guidance and insight might be made accessible to his conscious self. Divination, in this sense, is an art that builds a bridge between humanity and the gods, but, like all bridges, it should be passed over and not built upon.

Can the Tarot predict the future? Perhaps! The true answer, however, cannot be given so simply. If we recognize that, even though unconsciously, we are constantly shaping our future, it follows that by establishing a magical contact with our unconscious we can learn much about that future and, what is more, we can influence and alter it, thereby becoming, at least to a degree, masters of our own destiny. Time is a continuum, not a division, and its mysteries are often pierced when we recognize the proper significance of material clues to spiritual processes. Tarot divination is merely one particular application of these principles to the concerns of daily living.

How can we develop adequate skill in Tarot divination and at the same time steer free from the pitfalls of superstition? There are four cardinal requisites to proper and safe Tarot divination, and we shall briefly describe them here:

1. *The proper attitude,* which is to be found half-way between frivolity and superstitious awe, is the first requisite. The operation of divining with the Tarot is a serious business, for one does not call upon the gods in idle jest. At the same time, we must remember that the cards are only cards and by no means objects worthy of fear and veneration in themselves. Keeping the cards in precious containers, coloring them by hand, or burning candles before them will not alter the fact that they are pieces of cardboard, and no more. What matters is the psychological response the cards evoke from us; all else is of relatively small consequence.

2. *Adequate knowledge concerning the divinatory meaning of the cards* is the next requisite, and it is far more important than the average so-called psychic is willing to admit. One cannot practice divination merely by looking at the cards and "free associating" anything that enters one's mind. The Tarot is not a means of associative testing such as the Rorschach ink blots. One must memorize the basic symbolic and divinatory meanings of all seventy-eight cards before one can aspire to the status of a Tarot diviner. It is, of course, true that divination also includes the utilization of

unconscious material spontaneously surfacing in the diviner's mind during a reading, but such material must serve to amplify and not replace the art of interpreting the cards in terms of their accepted meaning.

3. *A natural talent for magical imagination* is another important requisite. It can be found in most people to some degree, and its growth within the individual psyche can be cultivated. Magical imagination is merely the ability to make the subjective or psychic reality relate itself meaningfully to the material clues at hand. The Tarot is certainly one of the very best means of stimulating this magical imagination, and the more we study and use it, the more we are apt to cultivate this important and exciting faculty.

4. *A willingness to face the hidden aspects of one's psyche* is the last, and probably the most important, requisite of all. No person suffering from the more severe forms of neuroses can practice any occult art without harming himself and others. The ancients had a saying that into an unprepared vessel the gods will pour their wine in vain. Those who have powerful demons lurking close to the threshold of their awareness might release them into manifestation within their personalities when engaged in the practice of the occult arts. Such unfortunate events do not discredit the Tarot or any other divinatory device; they merely reveal the ignorance of rushing in where angels fear to tread. Mercenary motives, as well as the desire for prestige and power through divination, are powerful hindrances to the success of a divinatory operation, for they tend to release undesirable psychological forces confusing the diviner. Tarot divination is serious business, not to be undertaken for mercenary or frivolous reasons. Such motives represent a profanation, not of the cards, but of the soul-power by which the cards are interpreted. When practiced by neurotics or persons of unworthy intentions, the divinatory art undergoes a degeneration, so that what was once a temple becomes a common marketplace in which thieves pursue their sinister trade and loafers idle away their time.

It is not wise to tempt the gods. Only when our minds fail to apprehend the graver issues of our lives, so that higher guidance alone can resolve our doubts and anxieties, is it advisable to resort to the divinatory offices of the Tarot. In all ordinary matters, common sense and logic are the natural judges and controllers, and only those issues that neither common sense nor reason can determine should become matters for the exercise of the high soul-faculty of divination.

The Tarot cards are windows into the inner chambers of the soul. Behind these windows hide the forces and images of past, present, and future; within the chambers dwell the gods and demons, figures of holy wisdom, and images of menace and madness. Still, there is no reason to fear the Tarot unless we interpret the word *fear* in the sense of fearing God, which truly means to revere and to approach with holy humility. As Eliphas Levi wrote more than a hundred years ago: "The Tarot is a veritable oracle and replies to all possible questions. This wheel (Tarot) is the real key to the Oratorical Art and the Grand Art . . . it is the true secret of the transmutation of shadows into light; it is the first and most important of all the arcana of the Great Work." Those who throughout the centuries have walked the path of wisdom and insight with this ancient picture book of Thoth as their companion would more than concur with Eliphas Levi in his paean of praise.

# MEDITATION *and*
# *the* TAROT

Human life has one purpose—to attain to union with God. It makes little difference whether this God be envisioned as personal or impersonal, or as a unity, a trinity, or an entire pantheon of personified divine powers. What matters is that human beings are capable of inwardly uniting themselves with a presence and a glory infinitely greater than their own human personalities; and that by realizing this potential, men and women can literally cease to be merely children of the earth and can join the kingdom of the gods, or of God.

The effort directed toward the objective of accomplishing this union has been known by many names: yoga, prayer, magic, and meditation. The latter has received much popular attention in recent years, unfortunately not always accompanied by an understanding of either the objective or the method involved. The purpose of meditation is to clear a pathway between the outer personality of the individual and the inner center of his being. This pathway becomes a Jacob's ladder upon which the ascending angels of the outer man meet and join in joyous union with the descending angels of the indwelling God. Ignorance, fear, hostility, guilt, and discord are the barriers that obstruct the freedom of the angelic host to meet at the summit of the soul. To learn the truth about our relationship to the godhead in our souls, and to shed the fetters that hold us captive, is to render us capable of traveling the pathway to Divinity at will. He who prays for anything but for union with God is a blasphemer!

The yogi whose exercises are directed toward an objective other than union with Brahman is but a false yogi. Similarly, all magic that does not aim at the invocation of Divinity into the magic circle of humanity is sorcery, and the same must be asserted about meditation. Health, wealth, love, happiness, and all the other treasures our personality desires are corrupted by the forces of the lower world. No prayer, yogic power, or magical privilege can alter the evanescence of earthly things. We must seek the kingdom that is not of this world, and, when we have discovered it, all things necessary and helpful to the welfare of our true selves will come to us in due course. He who meditates for "things" is both misguided and foolish, for he attempts to force the almighty Power to do the bidding of a puny, human ego, while at the same time assuming that he can escape the consequences of such an ill-advised act.

An ancient Chinese adept said: "If the wrong man uses the right means, the right means work in the wrong way." This saying stands in sad contrast to the all-too-frequent obsession of Westerners with the idea of the "right" method, irrespective of the character and motives of the one who applies it. The method is merely the path, the direction taken by the individual, but equally as important as the path is the individual himself. When preparing for the journey that is designed and ultimately destined to lead us beyond the stars, we must ask ourselves: What manner of person am I? If the honest answer is that we are fallible human souls, nevertheless desirous of recapturing our lost divinity, we shall find that almost any method of which we might avail ourselves will prove satisfactory. To the extent that we free ourselves from our frantic search for tricks and gimmicks—which might compensate for our wrong motives, our obtuseness, and our selfishness—we shall be led, at the proper time, to the suitable means that might aid us to pray, invoke, or meditate successfully.

Modern psychology, particularly in the researches of C. G. Jung, has found that Western consciousness suffers from what might be called the malady of one-sidedness. This ailment consists in our tendency to overvalue the conscious functions of our psychic being and neglect the unconscious portion. Modern science, and much that passes as "modern" religion, bears the baneful stamp of this excessive emphasis of the conscious ego at the expense of the unconscious self. The nature and function of all meditative efforts are very intimately related to this phenomenon, inasmuch as the objective of such efforts is clearly to be found in the unconscious selfhood of humankind.

The meditative effort, by whatever name it might be known, involves the assimilation of the unconscious component of our being. Among so-called "civilized" people, the overvaluation of the conscious psychic factor has become so great that the unconscious is forced into the background, and the personal ego becomes detached from the unconscious archetypes that are designed to act as links with the greater, cosmic, and mystical life. The human psyche is thus torn from its roots and no longer able to relate itself to the power and wisdom of the archetypal images. Striving for more and more conscious control over the forces and circumstances of life, the ego eventually loses control over itself, and neuroses and other afflictions make life unbearable.

Whether we say in religious terms that man must attain to union with God, or whether we assert with Jung that man must restore the archetypal realities to their rightful position in his psychic life, the task remains the same. Among the nonsense being disseminated in our day we find such statements as "Anyone can meditate" or "Just make your mind a blank." Without a considerable degree of ability to direct one's mind, no meditation is possible. This ability is difficult to acquire, and its effective cultivation is arduous at best. The ability to concentrate is an unavoidable precursor of any true meditation; without it, the student is likely to experience no more than a vague wandering of ideas and mental pictures. The subject of concentration immediately brings up the question of a suitable object. Some teachers advise people to concentrate on various commonplace things in no way related to any significant or inspiring concept, and thereby doom much commendable effort to failure due to a lack of motivation. Others will attempt to concentrate on a purely mental idea, while actually shutting their senses off, even to the extent of shutting their eyes.

Obviously, a way of meditation that would effectively combine the use of the senses with spiritually meaningful and helpful concepts and precepts would have great advantages over the practices noted above. Curiously enough, and unbeknownst to many, such a method of meditation exists and has been in use among Western occultists for centuries. It consists in a planned program of meditative exercises, using the twenty-two symbolic images of the Greater Trumps (Major Arcana) of the Tarot as the focal points of concentration.

In contrast with the majority of the Eastern schools of meditation, which tend to withdraw from the world of sense experience in a purely introspective manner, the Western esoteric tradition has always affirmed the value of the senses. The Masonic, Hermetic, Kabbalistic, and Rosicrucian symbolic philosophies, which constitute the mainstream of this tradition, have, for the most part, tended to utilize the senses as instrumentalities whereby higher states of consciousness and being might be attained. The sadly prevalent picture of the allegedly meditating devotee, with eyes tightly shut, a countenance devoid of all expression, the palms of the hands turned upwards in a queer gesture of receptive expectancy, as if some celestial chestnuts were to drop into them in short order—all of this appears most incongruous to the informed Western occultist. The image of the traditional adept of the mysteries is characterized by utmost alertness, concentration, a razor-sharp keenness of all senses, outer and inner. The master alchemist eagerly bending over his vessel or the ceremonial magician brandishing his wand in the center of the magic circle, are figures exuding *an active spirit* of striving for the supernal states of consciousness. This is not to say that the authentic exercises of Eastern yoga disciplines are characterized by the deplorable passivity alluded to above. What we object to here are the caricatures of Eastern meditation that are spread in our midst by those whom Jung called "pitiable imitators" of Eastern spiritual disciplines.

The use of the Tarot for the purpose of meditative activity is eminently compatible with this active spirit of the Western esoteric tradition. The unconscious thinks and acts in symbols and pictures. Thus, by utilizing a Tarot card as the focal point of our concentration, we have before us a picture filled with universal mystical and cosmic symbols. Far from being artificially contrived by artists working on the purely conscious level, these symbols are permanent denizens of the collective unconscious; they are not new acquaintances but old friends. Our soul is already familiar with the archetypal symbolism of the cards and, prompted by them, the recollection of the nature of the archetypal powers will reach the surface of our conscious mind once again. The followers of the Hindu Tantras, a school of mystical thought having much affinity with the Western occult tradition, have a saying that he who desires to raise himself up from the ground must do so with the aid of the ground. Sense experience is transcended and expanded into supersensual experience, not through passive introspection, but through the active application of soul power in the arena of the senses. It is through our senses that we can contemplate symbols that can then act as physical and mental footholds, so that consciousness can pass in an ordered manner from a symbol to a mystical principle. Understanding develops as the result of our increasing awareness of the relationship of symbol and principle.

Meditation with the aid of the Tarot is a helpful and valuable practice because it is founded on the experimental realities and laws of the human psyche. It is an active practice involving all components of the personality—physical, emotional, mental, and intuitive—without shutting any out. Also, it is a discipline developed by Western adepts over many centuries, thus having stood the test of time and experience. It requires no arduous physical exercises, no unnatural dietary rules, and no introduction of ascetic austerities into one's style of life. What it does require is a pure heart, an eager intellect, and an intuitive perception, all of which must be, and must remain, totally dedicated to the great objective of all meditation and of life itself: the effective union of the human personality with the indwelling Divine Presence, the Higher Self, the Daemonion, the Holy Guardian Angel, or whatever title we may bestow upon it.

# PATH WORK ALONG THE ROYAL ROAD

CHAPTER FOUR

# ℐ MAP *to the* KABBALAH *and the* MAJOR ARCANA

Our life proceeds in patterns. Extending through all states of existence we find a great system of patterns, a magic maze of paths and by-paths, of crossroads, blind alleys, and dead endings. Looking at our past history and present state as human beings, it seems apparent that our presence within, and our journeys upon, the roads of this pattern of life have not been particularly successful. Many spiritual systems have arisen throughout our evolutionary history, and all are intended to produce, or at least to intimate, a master pattern that might enable individual travelers to familiarize themselves with the terrain they are to traverse. Many attempts have been made to chart the map of the Divine Design. These attempts have been made by so many different means that the seeker today is likely to be bewildered by the profusion and confusion occurring among the charts and guidelines that offer themselves for potential use.

Amid the teachings and systems present in our age, there is one that merits more attention than it has so far received. This is the great symbolic glyph of the combined Tarot and the Kabbalah. At first glance, the very concept of regarding the two as a unified pattern, designed to aid substantially in the inner uplifting of man, appears preposterous. The Kabbalah is a collection of mystic-cosmic ideas concentrated in a symbolic design called the Tree of Life, which shows the way in which the unmanifest and infinite Being has taken on a finite and manifest aspect through emanation. It also shows how the finite manifestation may recover its original condition of infinity by retracing the steps of its forthcoming. The Tarot is ostensibly a deck of picture cards, used for a variety of purposes ranging from fortune-telling to gambling but apparently unsuited to the sublime nature and purposes of the Kabbalistic Tree of Life. Moreover, it is virtually impossible to establish with any degree of certainty that the symbolic systems of Kabbalah and Tarot had any relationship to each other until at least the eighteenth century—an exceedingly late date indeed to discover what purports to be an organic connection between two disciplines that coexisted side by side for many centuries. Academic historians, materialistic skeptics, and devout Hebrew Kabbalists, as well as a host of other critics, have for a long time condemned the combination of the Kabbalah and the Tarot into one unified system, as first openly accomplished by Eliphas Levi in the early nineteenth century and continued by modern occultists to the present day.

Eliphas Levi regarded the twenty-two cards of the Major Arcana (also known as the twenty-two Greater Trumps) as having unique mystic power to instruct and inspire the aspiring soul. He also noticed that the Tree of Life possesses twenty-two paths or channels, connecting the ten spheres or centers of emanated Divine Power (sephiroth) with each other and characterized by the twenty-two letters of the Hebrew alphabet. Critics observe with possible justification that the worthy Frenchman, being a romanticist, had simply mistaken a matter of coincidence for an organic and historical connection. To this objection, the mystical and magical scholars of France, as well as their English counterparts, replied that the connection between the Kabbalah and the Tarot was always known to certain initiates of the Hermetic and magical mysteries, but that it was simply not publicly revealed until the days of Eliphas Levi.

To the contemporary seeker after transcendental states of consciousness, these historical disputes are for the most part meaningless for two very good reasons. The first is that the combined system of the Kabbalah and the Tarot works. Whether the connection dates from the nineteenth century, or some century B.C., makes no difference to the considerable number of people who have experienced authentic reminiscences of their higher nature as the result of studying and meditating upon the Kabbalah in conjunction with the Tarot. The proof of the pudding is in the eating. Past history matters less than first-hand experience. The second reason in favor of the Kabbalah/Tarot combination may be found (not unlike so many other valuable truths) in the psychological teachings of C. G. Jung. In Jung's theory of synchronicity, we find the proposition that being coincidental does not negate the innate value of a fact. Coincidence, therefore, is no longer a dirty word, denoting a lack of meaningful relationship; far from it. Coincidence can be meaningful, and all the more meaningful, for the absence of the operation of causality. Applying this principle to our dilemma, we may state that whether the Tarot Arcana were ever applied to symbolize the twenty-two paths on the Tree of Life before Eliphas Levi or not makes no difference whatsoever. The coincidence of the two systems, if such it is, is not a mere haphazard concurrence of unrelated circumstances, but a meaningful coincidence of great psychological or, if you prefer, mystical power and purpose. Thus, from both the pragmatic and the psychological-theoretical point of view, the combined use of the Kabbalah and the Tarot appears fully justified.

Having thus disposed of the principal objection to our appointed task, we may turn our attention to these two symbolic systems. If it is our intention to meditate on the Tarot symbols in their relationship to the Kabbalah, we must be conversant with the main features of the Tree of Life itself. All authorities in the field of Kabbalistic meditation agree that unless the structure and attributions of the Tree of Life are firmly implanted in both the conscious and unconscious psyche of the student, meditation on the symbols will be without reward and, at times, might even prove counterproductive.

The Kabbalah, which represents a special transmission of soul wisdom outside of the canonical Holy Scriptures of Judaism, and which is possibly of non-Jewish origin, has as its central feature the unsurpassed universal symbol of the Tree of Life. This remarkable Design of Designs can be most effectively approached by describing it in three ways: (1) As a universal psychological Archetype as Such, as distinguished from an archetypal image. (In some of his later works, Jung made a distinction between archetypal images in the collective unconsciousness and Archetypes as Such, which he described as the sources of the archetypal images. Archetypes of this characterization are of sovereign numinosity and an unending fountainhead of power and inspiration to the outer man). (2) As a glyph of general applicability, upon which all aspects of experience, internal and external, can be placed and arranged in proper sequence and proper relationship. The Tree is likened in this respect to a filing system into which all experience and knowledge that comes our way may be deposited in an appropriate slot. (3) Lastly, but most importantly, the Tree must be recognized as being, not a system of information, but a method of using the mind or consciousness. It is this third definition that declares the suitability of the symbol of the Tree for the purpose of meditation.

The Tree of Life may also be said to reveal four great laws of universal being that apply as well to the human soul: (1) the Law of Emanation, which declares that all things are the successively emanated portions of the same divine essence; (2) the Law of Balance and Equilibrium, which states that life and growth imply balance, while imbalance leads to death and/or stagnation; (3) the Law of Unity in Diversity, reconciling the multiple emanations of the Tree with the monotheistic concept by stating that the essence is one, while its outpourings are many; and (4) the Law of the Ability to Return, according to which any manifestation of the emanated essence is capable of ascending to its own original source by climbing the paths and traversing the emanational centers (sephiroth) of the Tree. Kabbalistic meditation consists of effectively traveling along the branches of the Tree, up to and perhaps beyond the highest or crowning emanational center, the Sephira Kether.

The Tarot is in outward appearance a deck of cards, similar to any deck of playing cards—of which, in fact, it is the original form and prototype. One way of describing the full Tarot deck is to say that it consists of two packs in one, the larger of which, consisting of fifty-six cards, being known as the Minor Arcana, while the smaller, possessing twenty-two cards, being called the Major Arcana, or the Greater Trumps. Since the Minor Arcana, divided into four suits, may be taken symbolically to stand for the lower self or personality of man, this leaves the twenty-two cards of the Major Arcana as the symbols of the secret kingdom of the inner or Higher Self. Thus it is evident why the suit cards have been put to the personal and trivial use of gambling, while the symbolic cards of the Major Arcana became and remained a mystery to humanity, associated with magic and divination. It is this smaller pack, which in all existing decks consists of more or less identical figures, that serves as the visual group of symbols for Kabbalistic meditation within the tradition of the Western mysteries.

It was Eliphas Levi who described the Tarot as a philosophical mechanism that keeps the mind from wandering while leaving its initiative at liberty. It takes no imagination to recognize that he was referring to the use of the Tarot in meditation. By finding a useful way of correlating the cards of the Major Arcana with the paths which lead upward on the Tree of Life, we can easily and successfully put them to use by meditating on them in the sequence corresponding to the Tree's ascending paths and thus climb from its terrestrial base to its celestial crown. In order to do so with any degree of informed efficiency, it will be necessary to acquaint ourselves with the essentials of the emanational centers as well as with the paths of the Tree.

# The
# TEN WAY STATIONS

The Tree of Life is a symbolic representation of the relationships between the most abstract Being of Divinity and the most concrete existence of humanity. Since it is symbolic, we must gain some knowledge of the meaning and applications of its major symbols, especially as they pertain to the specific task of raising our own level of consciousness by way of meditating upon the Tarot Arcana. The grand symbol of the Tree serves several functions, some of which are philosophical-abstract, while others are practical-concrete.

Among the Tree's abstract or speculative uses is its ability to respond to the ever-timely question of philosophy: Whence have we come, and by what way, to our present habitat? To this question the Tree answers that we have come from the unmanifest, superessential state of preexistence and have descended by way of a process of emanation or outpouring. This flow from the unmanifest state of total abstraction proceeds in ten stages, each of which is likened to a vessel wherein the flowing essence enters, and, by overflowing, gives rise to a continued emanation, filling up the next vessel, all the way down to the lowest one, which stands for our present condition of embodied, concrete existence.

If, on the other hand, we ask another question: Where are we now, and how may we return to the condition from whence we came? the Tree will give us a somewhat different answer. We shall be told in this instance that we are in the sphere of manifestation, *Malkuth*, the "Kingdom," which consists of life in the world, and that we may recover our original estate by extending ourselves in mind, or consciousness, back along the same paths on which we traveled on our original journey down to materiality.

Obviously, the question for our present purpose is the latter one. On the one hand, for the purpose of general philosophical learning, it is quite proper to describe the Tree of Life, from top to bottom, in the order of the emanational sequence of the vessels, or as they are known, the "sephiroth." On the other hand, every little boy soon acquires the knowledge that he can only ascend a tree by climbing from branch to branch upward, starting at the very point where he finds himself when he begins to climb. Similarly, since we are embodied mortals desirous of recovering consciousness of ourselves as supernal beings, it will be necessary for us to learn about the Tree by ascending it, as if we were climbing from the earth to the Tree's crown. Thus we shall first turn our attention to the ten sephiroth in the order in which they will serve as way stations on our journey when, having picked ourselves up by our own spiritual bootstraps, we will have begun the climb to regain paradise.

The first way station we are concerned with is *Malkuth*, the "Kingdom." It is the psychological state of incarnate existence and the point where physical and spiritual forces touch each other. This state, we might say, is in fact where we are now. Just because we recognize this truth does not mean, however, that we are immediately ready to leap from the foot of the tree into the branches. Malkuth, our present condition, must first be explored and understood. This is where practical psychology and all devices conducive to personal self-understanding prove most useful. The four elements of Earth (Sensation), Water (Emotion), Fire (Thinking), and Air (Intuition) are the constituents of Malkuth. Unless we learn their laws and overcome their limitations, we shall not be ready to climb the tree.

The next way station at which we arrive is *Yesod*, the "Foundation." It is the seat of psychological forces directed toward biological functions, or at least always having a close relationship to such functions. The original, Freudian concept of the libido, or psychic energy centered mainly around the sexual instinct, is one of the main forces resident in Yesod. Thus, at this point, we must realize that psychic energy can be, and for our purpose sometimes must be, sublimated and diverted from purely instinctual expression in order to furnish us with the strength required to climb the Tree.

*Hod*, or " Splendor" or "Glory," is the name of the next stopping point, if we follow the original sequence of emanations in reverse (although it is likely that on our return journey we shall first actually make contact with another, i.e. *Netzach*, "Victory"). In Hod we must recognize the spiritual essence, or evolutionary potential, of our mind, or thinking principle. While the *function* of thinking in its operative sense is within the sphere of Malkuth, the *principle* of mind is associated with Hod. The mind has rightly been called the slayer of the real, for it is through the divisive, katabolic power of thinking that the unitary quality of life is fragmented as the holy essence descends into manifestation. Conversely, this same mind can be the restorer of the real if we recognize its potential to redeem us from emotional attachments and false values.

Our attention now turns to the way station represented by *Netzach*, or "Victory," and characterized by feeling, or emotion. The same forces that in Malkuth are expressed as activity, in Yesod as vitality, and in Hod as mentality are manifest in Netzach as sentiment and even sentimentality. This station is on the same level as Hod, indicating that here also we are faced with an instrument that can work for our involution or for our evolution, and that the choice is strictly up to us. If we love God above all else, then our feelings will serve the purpose of our reunion with our Father who is in heaven; but if we turn the force of our emotions to earthly objectives, we shall be tied to the earth as with a thousand chains. The proper ordering of emotional priorities must be accomplished at this point of the journey.

*Tiphareth*, or "Beauty," is the name of the next way station, and it is indeed the most beautiful of all the stations we shall travel through. At the very center of the Tree, it is the principal center of inner gravity of our own selves. Since balance and equilibrium are the supreme virtues of the Kabbalah and this station is the most perfectly balanced of the ten sephiroth, it is a state the loveliness of which defies description. It is also the apex of our human nature

43

and the meeting point of the human and the Divine. Tiphareth could be likened to the summit of Mt. Sinai, where Moses, the representative of humanity, met with God and received His Laws. It is the most elevated state of consciousness of which the human being is capable.

The next stop—namely, the stern and powerful sephirah *Geburah*, "Severity" or "Justice"—contrasts sharply with the balanced and pleasant beauty of Tiphareth. We have now passed personal limits and have joined the world of superhuman potencies. Therefore, we must prove strong and wise enough to face the fears and problems of the full force of retributive justice, sometimes called "karma" in modern occult parlance. We now recognize that having outgrown our humanity in Tiphareth was not our true goal at all and that we are still only half-way to reaching our actual objective, the essential divinity of Kether. Were it not for the memory of the balanced state of the previous way station, the experience of which must now be part of our being, we should assuredly perish under the scourge and hammer of almighty Geburah.

The terrors of Geburah are balanced and ameliorated by our next stop, *Chesed*, "Mercy" (at times also called *Gedulah*, "Love"). This is our great comforter, who wipes away all tears from our eyes and in whose benevolent house we find comfort, rest, and refreshment. Like a warm, cheerful inn, this station restores our strength and permits us to gird our loins for the further climb upward. When we traverse this sphere, we know without any shadow of doubt that every cloud has a silver lining indeed and that, when "the Lord giveth and the Lord taketh away," His giving always and fully compensates for His taking.

Justice and Mercy, the two side pillars of the Tree, are represented in equal proportion; therefore, at this point we can love much and wisely at the same time. While this level is assuredly the apex of human attainment, the Kabbalah teaches us that there are as many superhuman potentialities within us as there are human ones, and therefore we must go on.

The sephirah *Binah*, "Understanding," is the first station among what are called the Supernal Spheres. This region is not only superhuman, but totally beyond all comprehension from any level ordinarily accessible to humanity. In short, it is the province of what religion calls God. Still, in a purely subjective and extremely cautious way, we can make some tentative statements about these spheres, though these statements must be recognized as illusory at best. The altering of consciousness necessary in order to deal with the conditions of the Supernals is so great that it passes our ability to imagine. Binah is often called the Supernal Mother. If there be any useful correlation between the Christian Trinity and the three Supernal Sephiroth of the Tree, Binah might correspond to the Holy Ghost who, like a mother, is the giver of life. But since giving life in involution implies limitation, Binah has a generally saturnine and restricting aspect. It is the hand of God that tends to take away.

*Chokmah*, "Wisdom," is the second Supernal Sphere, and our next-to-the-last way station. Ultimate benevolence, expressed as true wisdom, is its chief characteristic. It is the last quality we can be said to gain before we attain to complete union with the godhead. This wisdom is not learning, memory, talent, or an aggregation of mental force. It is the full potential of creative energy, expressed as all-knowing, all-planning, all-resolving wisdom. If there be any quality recognized in this region beyond all qualities, it would be that of infinite expansion, or the ability to attain to "oceanic consciousness," wherein we are merged with all and wisely comprehend all.

*Kether*, the "Crown," is the ultimate summit of the Tree, and, in a way, of all that is. This is the treetop. It is both the crown of the kingly being that is the Tree and the crowning height of our journey. The prodigal son has now reached the house of his father. The dewdrop from the earth has slipped into the shining sea. Beyond this point there is only silence and the mysterious radiance of impenetrable darkness. The immeasurable may not be measured with thoughts and words, but the testimony of the wise and holy souls in every age assures us that it can be experienced.

CHAPTER SIX

# The
# TWENTY-TWO HIGHWAYS

After having considered the ten way stations of our journey, it is necessary for us to turn our attention to the twenty-two highways, or roads, that interconnect them. The word *path*, traditionally used to describe these connections, is somewhat misleading, unless we understand the peculiar nomenclature employed by the early Kabbalists. In one of the ancient standard works on the Kabbalah, the *Sepher Yetzirah*, all aspects of the Tree are called "paths"—the "Thirty-two Paths of Concealed Glory"—so that the ten spheres of manifestation (sephiroth) are known as the first ten paths, and the twenty-two connections between these are numbered eleven through thirty-two. In spite of this deceptive numeration, we must remember that the paths proper are the connecting links between the ten sephiroth.

In order to distinguish the sephiroth from the paths proper, it is necessary to make a qualitative distinction between the two. The ten sephiroth represent relatively objective states of consciousness or stable modifications of psychic energy, while the paths stand for subjective experiences that the individual psyche undergoes while its consciousness is being transferred from one sephirah, or state, to another. An analogy, necessarily inadequate, might be the envisioning of each sephirah as a town or city wherein the traveler may tarry for a while, while the paths might be viewed as highways designed for continuous movement as the wayfarer moves from one locale to another. The ten way stations are characterized by a relatively static condition of psychic energy, while the chief attribute of the highways joining them together is that of progression, movement, and dynamic energy. Using the analogy of language, we could liken the sephiroth to nouns, words denoting being, and the paths as verbs, words denoting action. Thus our designations as way stations and highways could be amplified and at the same time found sufficient.

The symbolism of the paths is threefold, each having assigned to it the following: (1) a letter of the Hebrew alphabet, which has twenty-two letters; (2) an astrological attribution, such as a planet or a sign of the Zodiac; and most importantly (3) a Tarot Trump, or card of the Major Arcana. Of these three, almost certainly the first—i.e., the Hebrew letter attribution—is the oldest and, in the eyes of the traditional Kabbalists, the most meaningful. The Hebrew letters were regarded as sacred manifestations of the power of the godhead. Their very shapes and sequence were considered to hold most potent divine secrets. The letters are assigned to the paths in descending order from the top down, and they are enumerated in reverse on the upward course we are to follow in our meditations. The astrological attributions are also of great antiquity, although some modifications have been recently introduced. At one time, when only seven planets were known, in addition to their seven planetary signs and the twelve signs of the Zodiac, three of the four elemental symbols were included; namely, Air, Water, and Fire. Some of the more recent contemporary Kabbalists have replaced these elements with the planets Uranus, Pluto, and Neptune, which had not yet been discovered in the days of the ancient Kabbalists. (The total of the ancient seven and the more newly-discovered three planets seems contrary to the *astronomical* total of nine, unless we realize that the *astrological* scheme also classifies the Moon as a planet.)

For our purposes, the most significant of the attributive systems is that involving the Tarot Trumps. The true attributions have been and are a source of controversy among the scholars of Tarot and Kabbalah. Without wasting precious time on these arguments, we shall merely mention that there are two main systems of attributing the Tarot Trumps to the paths. The first of these—originated by Eliphas Levi and still adhered to by the French school of

occultists, including Papus and, more recently, Mouni Sadhu—
does not place the Trump numbered zero at the beginning of the
sequence of paths, but rather incomprehensibly inserts it between
the twenty-first and twenty-second card at the bottom of the Tree.
In contradistinction to this system, the more popular method is
that of the once illustrious Order of the Golden Dawn, which more
logically places zero before one and assigns the Fool to the first
path proper (technically known as the Eleventh Path), and from
hence proceeds in the regular order from one to twenty-one. One
might be tempted to observe that the entire problem originates
with the curious circumstance that the twenty-two Trumps are
numbered, not one through twenty-two, but rather zero through
twenty-one, which gives occasion for disagreement. In our present
treatise of meditations, we shall follow the Golden Dawn system of
attributions, the basic validity of which will seem self-evident to
anyone who uses it as a method of expanding awareness instead of
as a mere exercise of the intellect. We shall also abstain from engag-
ing in any of the further modifications introduced into the Golden
Dawn system by later students, such as the reversal of the positions
on the Tree of the cards of the Emperor and the Star.

In addition to the three major attributions of the Hebrew
letters, astrological signs, and Tarot Trumps, numerous minor
attributive efforts exist, in the course of which we may find colors,
gems, metals, herbs, perfumes, animals, and magic weapons—as
well as Egyptian, Greek, and Nordic gods—assigned to each of the
paths. All are useful from a psychological point of view, inasmuch
as they offer the student additional points of reference designed to
illumine the character and nature of the path one wishes to traverse. Thus, one student may be susceptible to the symbolic language of astrology, while another may respond to the symbols of
alchemy, and yet another's comprehension may be stimulated by
the figures of the gods of ancient religions. The more aids we can
enlist to serve our purpose, the greater the likelihood of safely traveling upon the paths. Each symbolic system could be likened to a
small candle, or light bulb, used to illumine our way. The more
sources of light we possess, the less likely we shall be to end up in a

ditch instead of at our destination. In the following discussion, therefore, we shall mention very briefly most of these attributions without, however, explaining them further, thus allowing students to use these potential keys to unlock the chambers of their understanding in accordance with the special demands of their own background and inclination.

The first grouping of paths, or highways, leading from earth to heaven may be called the "Paths of the Personality" and consists of the following:

We begin our journey on the *Thirty-second Path*, which leads from the sephirah Malkuth to the next highest sephirah, Yesod. Psychologically, it indicates the transferring of consciousness from bodily form to psychophysiological energy. In it is involved the transmuting of the static energy of the body to the dynamic energy of the psyche, the latter being vaguely analogous to the libido of Freudian psychology. Attributed to this path are the Hebrew letter *Tav*, the T-shaped cross that indicates the ability of spirit to escape from matter; the somber planet Saturn, symbolic of restriction; and the Tarot Trump named the World. Further attributions are the color indigo and the gem onyx. The animal is the crocodile; the plants are ash and cypress; the science is alchemy; the magical weapon is the Sickle; the perfume is frankincense; and the divinities are Saturn, Brahma, Nephtys, and Athena.

The next in order is the *Twenty-ninth Path*, leading from Malkuth to Netzach. Joining the physical consciousness with the emotional nature, it signifies the emergence of extremely powerful, and sometimes baneful, unconscious complexes. Since the intellectual clarifying force of Hod has not been touched yet, these unconscious forces are encountered without understanding, and thus confusion and apprehension may result. On this path the aspirant is beginning to deal with the "shadow" conceptualized in Jungian psychology; that is, with his own repressed counterpart. The associated letter is *Quoph*, referring to the back of the head. The astrological sign is Pisces (and less frequently the Moon). The Tarot Trump is also the Moon, depicting an eerie scene by moonlight. The color is violet; the plants are poppy, hibiscus, and nettle; the gem is chrysolight; the animal is the dolphin; the perfume, amber-gris; and the magical weapon, a Magic Mirror. Narcotic drugs also belong here, as well as the gods Vishnu, Neptune, and Poseidon.

The *Thirty-first Path*, proceeding from Malkuth to Hod, follows. Its keynote is the renewal of one's total being through the power of the intellect. After having begun with Form, we have touched the Life Force, then Feeling, and at this point add Thinking, whereby great changes may occur in our nature. The letter *Shin*, meaning a "tooth," is given to this path. The planet is Pluto, and the card is called Judgement. The color is scarlet red tinged with orange; opal is the precious stone; the animal is the lion; the plant is the hibiscus; the magical weapons are the Wand and Lamp; and the perfume is olibanum. The gods attached to this path are Pluto, Hades, and Horus.

Next is the *Thirtieth Path*, connecting Yesod with Hod. The energy of vitality, joined with the light of the intellect, is likely to produce much light upon all subjects, as well as much warmth, which will make for growth and psychological fertility or creativity. The danger attendant upon this path is overconfidence—too great a reliance on the mind. The letter is *Resh*, referring to the front of the head. The astrological valuation is the Sun, while the Tarot Trump is also called the Sun. The color is orange; heliotrope is the gem; the plant is the sunflower; the animal is the sparrow hawk; the magical weapons are the Bow and Arrow; the perfume is cinnamon; the drug is alcohol; and the gods are Surya, Apollo, Helios, and Ra.

The *Twenty-eighth Path*, leading from Yesod to Netzach, is characterized by the flow of vitalizing energy toward the feeling nature. The basic instability of the emotions can be overcome with the vital strength. This path should not be traveled until after the sephirah Hod has been touched via one of the paths; otherwise, the energy flowing into the emotional nature might lead to undesirable excesses of passion. The letter is *Tzaddi*, a "fishhook," the astrological significator is the sign of Aquarius. The Tarot Trump is known as the Star (although some students, following theoretician of magic Aleister Crowley, use the Emperor). The color is red-purple;

the jewel is the crystal; the plant the olive; the animal the peacock; the perfume galbanum; the magical weapon the Censer; and the divinities Juno and Athena.

The *Twenty-seventh Path*, which runs horizontally across the Tree joining Hod and Netzach, follows. It is known as the first veil or barrier on the upward path, and it is full of peril and destructive potential. Joining intellect with feeling, its experience resembles that of mixing fire with water, which generates steam, a source of great power for better or for worse. The paths leading up to this point may be visualized as the supporting beams of a scaffolding upon which consciousness now may walk across, precariously balanced. The letter *Peh*, meaning "mouth," as well as the warlike planet Mars, are assigned to this path. The Tarot Trump is the Tower, also known as the Lightning Struck Tower and the House of God. The color is scarlet, the gem is the ruby, the plants are absinthe and rue, and the animals are the bear and the wolf. The magical weapon is the Two-edged Sword, the perfume is pepper, and the gods are Mars and Ares.

At this point we have exhausted what might properly be called the paths of the personality or of the lesser self. The highways now to be traversed represent links with our higher nature, as exemplified by the sephirah Tiphareth, the intuitive principle of balanced love and willing sacrifice. By climbing to Tiphareth, the soul is like Moses ascending Mt. Sinai to converse with God. Thus the paths now to be described are the "Paths of Individuality" or of the Higher Self.

The first of these is the *Twenty-fifth Path*, leading from Yesod to Tiphareth. This is the first path of divine illumination, wherein the individual experiences contact with the indwelling god, the Christ within, the hope of glory, the Holy Guardian Angel. It is a path of great energy, and, significantly, it proceeds from the sephirah of vital force, which also is the first operative center of the psychosexual power, sometimes called "Kundalini." If the aspirant has not completed the paths of the personality prior to this experience, the aroused fire might easily injure and even destroy him. The letter is *Samech*, meaning a "prop." The astrological sign is

Sagittarius (being the arrow, propelled by the bow, which is composed of the Thirtieth, Twenty-eighth, and Twenty-seventh Paths). The Tarot Trump is called Temperance, depicting a fiery angel engaged in the mixing (tempering) of diverse elements. Blue is the color, jacinth the gem, and rush the plant. The animals are the horse and dog, the magical weapon is the Arrow, the perfume is aloes, and the goddesses are Diana and Artemis.

The *Twenty-sixth Path*, connecting Hod and Tiphareth, is next. The divine illumination of Tiphareth spells doom to the rule of the intellect; therefore, this path is arduous and painful. The escape from the limitations of form is not without its trials. The letter is *Ayin*, meaning the "eye"; the astrological sign is Capricorn, the goat climbing hazardous mountains. The Trump is called the Devil and is modeled on the Goat of Mendes. Black, flecked with indigo, is the color; the black diamond is the gem; hemp and thistle are the plants; and the goat and the ass are the animals. The magical weapon is the Lamp, the perfume is musk, and the gods are Pan and Set.

Corresponding to the previous path, but on the opposite side of the Tree, we come upon the *Twenty-fourth Path*, leading from Netzach to Tiphareth. Just as the tyranny of the intellect is abolished by the advent of the illumination bestowed by Tiphareth, so in this case the advent of the Tipharetic Kingdom sounds the death knell to the rule of the passions. All that is not worthy to enter the Kingdom must die so that it might come to life in a new, purified form. The destruction of the egotistical drives and feelings for the purpose of psychological reconstruction on a higher level of individuation is accomplished on this path. The letter is *Nun*, meaning a "fish," and the astrological sign is Scorpio, having to do with death and regeneration. The Tarot Trump is number thirteen, a number of fatality, and is named Death. Sometimes this card depicts the traditional figure of the grim reaper and sometimes, an armored, mounted skeleton. The color is blue-green, the gem is the snakestone, the plant is the cactus, and the animals are the scorpion and the wolf. The perfume is opoponax; the magical weapon is the Pain of Obligation; and the gods are Mars, Ares, and Kephra.

The paths leading from Tiphareth to the higher sephiroth, while within the structure of the individuality, or Higher Self, are yet further to be distinguished by what might be called their initiatory or adeptic nature. Tiphareth is the apex of human nature as we know it. It is the point that, if transcended, makes us more than human. This entry into a superhuman region, which is not yet fully divine but nevertheless godlike, has been named initiation. Those who have entered these paths are known as initiates, or adepts, who have become adept in the art of overcoming their own human limitations. Thus, the following paths are called the "Paths of Adeptship."

The first of these is the *Twenty-second Path*, leading from Tiphareth to Geburah; that is, from psychological balance to the severe judgment seat of the higher conscience. Now we feel the full pain of the sacrifice offered by the soul on the altar of Tiphareth, and the weight of the law descends in a sometimes-oppressive fashion. Clarity of judgment—the combination of beauty with rectitude and equity—is required on this path. The letter is *Lamed*, meaning an "ox-goad"; the astrological attribution is that of the sign of Libra; and the Tarot Trump is named Justice. The color is emerald green; the precious stone is the emerald; the animal is the elephant; the perfume is galbanum; the plant is the aloe; the drug is tobacco; and the gods are Yama, Vulcan, Ma, and Maat.

The *Twentieth Path*, joining Tiphareth with Chesed, is next. Linking balanced consciousness with higher love, it is a path of great peace but also of solitude. Leaving all attachments behind, the soul engages in the "flight of the alone to the alone." By following in the footsteps of the adepts who have gone before, we in our turn become way showers to those who will follow. The letter is the mysterious *Yod*, often indicating the seed or beginning of life, and literally meaning "an open hand." The astrological sign is Virgo. The Trump is the Hermit. The color is yellowish-green, the gem is the peridot, and the plants are the snowdrop and the lily. Solitary animals, such as the rhinoceros, are said to relate to this path. The Wand and the Lamp are the magical weapons, and the perfume is that of the narcissus. All anaphrodisiacs are considered drugs appropriate to this path, and the divinities are Ceres, Shiva in his yogi aspect, Attis, and Isis.

The *Nineteenth Path*, or the second barrier or cross path that runs between Chesed and Geburah, is the one we travel on next. The force of the sublimated beast, the raised psychosexual force, is now employed in bridging the gap between the two great opposites of Mercy and Severity. The great alchemical work of uniting sulphur and salt and the light and dark halves of the soul, Yin and Yang, is to be accomplished on this path. The letter is *Teth*, meaning a "serpent," suggestive of the serpent power of Kundalini. The astrological sign is Leo, and the Trump is called Strength. The color is yellow with greenish and purple shading. The gem is the cat's-eye, the plant is the sunflower, and the animal is the lion. The magical weapon is Discipline; the perfume is olibanum; the drugs are the carminatives; and the gods are Venus, Vishnu, and Demeter.

The *Twenty-third Path* that follows is the first side path we encounter on our upward journey, connecting Hod to Geburah. It is to be found entirely on one column, without any balancing influence from anywhere else. The intellectual principle is connected to a rather merciless spiritual faculty of judgment on this path, and the qualities are appropriate. Here it is necessary to sacrifice all of our previous ideas and standards; otherwise, we shall be turned back. The letter is *Mem*; that is, the "seas" or "water." The modern astrological attribution is the planet Neptune, while anciently it was merely the element of water. The Tarot Trump is the Hanged Man, depicting a person suspended upside down. The color is deep blue and the gem, the beryl. The lotus and other water plants belong here. The animals are the eagle and the scorpion, the magical weapons are the Cup and the Cross, the perfume is myrrh, the drugs are sulphates and cascara, and the gods are Neptune and Poseidon.

Corresponding to the foregoing, but located on the opposite pillar, we find the *Twenty-first Path*, leading from Netzach to Chesed. Moving from the sphere of Venus, the lesser fortune, Netzach, to the sphere of ultimate benevolence, Chesed, we may count ourselves fortunate, indeed. On this path, the energies of the psyche seem to propel us from one good fortune to an even greater one. Still, it is incumbent upon us to remember that its benevolent aspects will hold good only so long as we continue to maintain ourselves in a state of balance and equilibrium, keeping the four elements of personal selfhood—sensation, emotion, intellect, and intuition—properly balanced. This is the path of great opportunity, but we must remind ourselves that it is far better to be prepared for opportunity than to seek it. The letter associated with this path is *Kaph*, meaning an "open hand"; the planet is the munificent Jupiter; and the Tarot Trump is the Wheel of Fortune. Royal violet is the color; the gems are amethyst and lapis lazuli; the plants are hyssop, oak, poplar, and the fig tree; the animal is the eagle; the perfume is saffron; the magical weapon is the Scepter; the drug is cocaine; and the gods are Jupiter, Pluto, Zeus, and Amon-Ra.

The following paths are once again distinguished from the preceding ones, inasmuch as they serve to join the sephiroth of exalted humanity, Tiphareth, and semidivinity, Geburah and Chesed, with those of the triune godhead: Binah, Chokmah, and Kether. The five paths we shall deal with now, therefore, might properly be named the "Paths of Greater Initiation," or the "Paths of the Spirit."

The path beginning this group is the *Thirteenth Path*, leading from Tiphareth to Kether. It is the longest, and possibly the most perilous, of all the paths, but it is also the most beautiful and mysterious. From the apex of human existence it proceeds straightway into the abode of the highest principle of the godhead itself. The only reason for its ability to accomplish this unbelievable task is that it is the path of ultimate balance, the last portion of the path of the arrow, which began with the Thirty-second Path, continued with the Twenty-fifth, and concludes in this, the Thirteenth. In theory, it would be possible for the soul to travel on this central course only, without touching any of the other paths, but this possibility is minimal and fraught with extreme danger. The temptation may be great to attempt the journey to Kether immediately upon our arrival at Tiphareth; but without the strengthening and balancing influence of Geburah and Chesed, as well as of the paths leading to them, we would assuredly perish upon the Thirteenth Path and plunge into the dread abyss which separates the world of the godhead—the three Supernal Sephiroth of Binah, Chokmah, and Kether—from the human and semidivine regions. The aspirant thus must resist the temptation to attempt a merging of consciousness with the ultimate godhead immediately upon reaching the first authentic divine illumination. Shortcuts are, for the most part, incompatible with lasting progress and extremely hazardous at best. The letter given to the Thirteenth Path is *Ghimel*, meaning "camel": the astrological attribution is the Moon; and the Tarot Trump is the second numbered card of the Major Arcana, called the High Priestess. The great journey to God, therefore, is often portrayed as being undertaken on the back of a camel, crossing the perilous desert at night, led by the mysterious light of the moon. Blue is the color; the gems are moonstone and pearl; the animal is the dog; the plants are hazel, moonwort, and ranunculus; the magical weapon is once again the Bow and Arrow; the perfumes are camphor and aloes; the drugs are juniper and pennyroyal; and some of the deities, among others, are Chomse, Artemis, Hecate, and Diana, as well as the Virgin Mary.

The *Seventeenth Path*, leading from Tiphareth to Binah, is the next to be traveled. It proceeds from the position of balance to the dark, restrictive apex of the negative pillar. It is a path wherein the element of right choices and proper priorities is of extreme importance. Were it not for the temporary union with the ultimate godhead experienced at the end of the preceding Thirteenth Path, the traveler might be most adversely affected by his entry into the sphere of Binah at the end of the present path. This is primarily a path of choices. The quality to be developed and depended upon here is discrimination, or discerning judgment. Unless the traveler maintains his balance within his own nature, by way of a proper ordering of his inward priorities, he may plunge down through Tiphareth to the lower paths of probation. If the path is successfully completed, it will raise the soul to the consciousness of Binah, and it will be reborn into the life of God, by reentering the dark womb of the Divine Mother. The letter attributed to this path is

*Zayn,* meaning "sword," and the Tarot Trump is the Lovers, which is the sixth card of the Major Arcana. The Greek word for six is *hex,* and the Latin word is *sex,* all of which serves to corroborate that the duality of the psychosexual forces plays an important role on this path, and also that magic, or sorcery, is a potential hazard at this juncture. The Zodiacal sign is Gemini, the predominant color is orange, precious stones are tourmaline and the alexandrite, the plant is the orchid, and the animal is the magpie. The drug is ergot, which contains the psychedelic drug LSD, and the perfume is wormwood. The magic weapon is the Tripod, and the gods are Castor and Pollux—as well as other twin deities—and Apollo the Diviner.

Next follows the *Fifteenth Path,* leading from Tiphareth to Chokmah. Like the preceding one, this path also runs across the abyss and crosses over the middle pillar. This trajectory renders it hazardous, but not quite so much as the Seventeenth Path, since it culminates in the benevolent forces of wisdom as embodied in Chokmah. It is one of the major paths of initiation trod by high adepts. The letter *Heh* belongs on this path, meaning a "window." The astrological attribution is Aries, and the card is the Emperor. The color is scarlet red, and the gem is the ruby. The plants are the tiger lily and the geranium; the animals are the ram and the owl. The magical weapons associated with this path are the Horns, Energy, and the Burin. The perfume is dragon's blood; the drugs are all cerebral excitants; and the gods are Mars, Minerva, Shiva, and Athena.

The next to be traveled is the *Eighteenth Path,* which runs from Geburah to Binah. It is located entirely on the pillar of restriction, or severity. In consequence, it is a path of extreme power, but having the qualities of rigorousness, strictness, and mercilessness. Unlike the Seventeenth Path, this one does not possess the softening influence of Tiphareth and is therefore a hard and terrible road to travel. On it, the wayfarer must learn the correct use of power and be mindful of the qualities of the previously traversed Thirteenth Path with its experience of Kether and the sacrificial love of Tiphareth; otherwise, he will fall victim to the experience of unmitigated dominance. The letter of this path is *Cheth*, meaning a "fence"; the astrological attribution is the cruel and forceful sign of Cancer; and the Tarot Trump is called the Chariot. The color is amber, and the precious stone is that of the same name. The plant is the lotus, the animals are the crab and the turtle, the magical weapon is the Fiery Furnace, the perfume is onycha, and the herbal drug is watercress. The gods are Mercury, Apollo the Charioteer, and Khephra.

The *Sixteenth Path*, connecting Chesed and Chokmah, and thus entirely located on the giving, mild pillar, is next. Here we travel from love to wisdom. In appearance, this path seems milder and more joyous than the preceding Eighteenth, but in reality it is also a path of much loneliness and sorrow. On it, the traveler must learn how to wed wisdom and love and thereby serve humanity in an utterly impersonal way. It is the path of religiously oriented initiation, and its function is to transform the initiate into an initiator. The Hebrew letter is *Vav*, meaning a "peg" or "nail." The astrological attribution is Taurus, and the Tarot Trump is called the Hierophant. The color is red-orange, the precious stone is topaz, the plant is mallow, and the animal is the bull. The magical weapon is the Labor of Preparation; the perfume is storax; the drug is sugar cane; and the gods are Venus, Apis, Osiris, and Hera.

Three more highways remain to be traveled at this juncture, and since they serve exclusively to interconnect the way stations (sephiroth) of the godhead—namely, the Supernal Triad of Kether, Chokmah, and Binah—they may be justly called the "Paths of Divinity." They are the following:

The *Fourteenth Path*, which runs from Binah to Chokmah, represents the love of the Supernal Father for the Supernal Mother, and vice versa. It is the last horizontal path or barrier upon the Tree, and thus it also represents a certain hazard or danger connected with what we must call the "law of generation," as contrasted with the "law of regeneration." The downward path from the crown of the Tree to its base is under the law of generation; that is, its purpose is the manifesting of objective reality from the original state of subjective being. On the other hand, the objective of the upward journey is the realization of being and the detachment of the individual consciousness from its attachment to objectivity. The motherly Fourteenth Path thus serves two separate and opposite objectives, depending on whether it is traveled downward or upward. On the path of forthcoming, it becomes the mother-force of generation, or the root of creating objective beings and conditions to which we might become attached. On the path of return, we are being given birth in an intangible, subjective sense; we become born as children of the Divine. Thus we find the ultimate union of the highest archetypal realities of what C. G. Jung called the "anima" and the "animus," referring to the inner feminine aspect of a man and to the inner masculine aspect of a woman, respectively. At this point, we ourselves become the spiritual offspring of the *mysterium coniunctionis*, the Hermetic marriage of this last great pair of opposites. We must guard our step, however, so that the titanic force of love encountered here will not flow in the direction of earthly pursuits and reverse our direction of travel at this late stage. The letter given to this path is *Daleth*, meaning a "door," since it serves as the doorway between the unmanifest and the manifest. The astrological planet is Venus, and the Tarot Trump is the beautiful and matronly figure of the Empress. The color is emerald green, and the gems are the emerald and the turquoise. Myrtle, rose, and clover are the plants; and the animals are the sparrow, dove, and swan. The magical weapon is the Girdle or Belt. The perfumes are sandalwood and myrtle; the drugs are love philtres. The gods are Venus, Lalita, Aphrodite, and Freya.

The next highway to be traveled is known as the *Twelfth Path*, which joins Binah and Kether. It joins the fountain of the form side of being, Binah, with the undifferentiated existence of Kether, wherein the polarities of form and life, negative and positive, and female and male are one. On this path we are called to perform the supreme magical task of transforming matter into energy, form into substance, and mind into the root of mind. The four elements of earth, water, fire and air, after being ordered into a harmonious system of a working pattern, are now drawn up into the ineffable force of the Supreme. Within the individual, this process means the recovery of the transpersonal essence of the constituent functions of personal consciousness. We penetrate to the mysterious core of the experiences offered to us through sensation, emotion, thinking, and intuition. Supreme illumination of the mind takes place as the faculty of understanding, Binah, penetrates into the crowning consciousness of the godhead. Just as the noonday sun changes the water of the earth into vapor and thus draws this essence into itself, so on this path the supercelestial power of Kether draws unto itself the essence of the form side of emanated being from the dark pillar of severity through Binah, its apex. The bodily assumption of the Divine Mother, in Christian dogma, is a concept closely allied to the upward travel on this path, since it symbolizes the upliftment and ultimate transformation of the form-and-birth-giving principle of creation. The dogma of the Assumption of the Virgin Mary, proclaimed by Pope Pius XII, was considered to be of crucial psychological importance for Christianity by Jung, who hailed it as a sign of the new aeon of Aquarius.

The path of the transformation of form into energy has its attendant hazards. In certain ways it might be likened to the process of liberating the power of the atom: it may be productive of great destruction if wrongfully applied. It is imperative that the traveler should have assimilated into his experience the qualities of both Chesed and Chokmah when he ventures on this path, lest the titanic power of impersonal energy blast him out of the Tree of Life and turn him into a solitary power, gloriously but fruitlessly enthroned outside the divine emanational pattern. In this respect it must be remembered, and indeed most emphatically recalled, that the objective of Kabbalistic meditative work is not our departure from manifestation, but our effective and enlightened continued presence therein. The Kabbalist usually does not strive for liberation from life but rather hopes to become one with life itself, so as to have and give life more abundantly. In this respect, such an individual resembles the Bodhisattva of Mahayana Buddhism, who takes the great vow to assist in the enlightenment of all creatures in preference to personal liberation from manifest existence. Using the Buddhist analogy, the adept, lacking balance by way of Chesed and Chokmah, could easily become a Pratyeka Buddha, or a Solitary Enlightened One, whose orbit has left that of the divine system of life and redemption. It is thus that only the consciousness filled and enlightened with love and mercy can properly administer the raw force of impersonal power.

The Hebrew letter given to this path is *Beth*, meaning a "house." The planet Mercury is attributed to it, and the Tarot Trump is the Magician. The color is a pure yellow, the precious stones are the opal and the agate, the animals are the swallow and the ape. The magical weapon is the Caduceus; the perfumes are mastic, mace, and storax; vegetable drugs are vervain and herb mercury. The gods associated with this path are Mercury, Thoth, Hermes, and Cynocephalus.

One path only remains, and it is the most glorious, mysterious, and paradoxical of all. It is the *Eleventh Path*, which joins Chokmah and Kether. This is in very truth the point of all beginnings and all endings; for it is upon this path that the first flash of the fiery lightning of manifestation comes forth at the beginning of each and every cycle of emanation; and it is also at this point that the returning sap of the Tree is finally and completely joined with the ultimately equilibrated beginning and end of all. When the wisdom that is perfect love is united in complete balance with the understanding of perfect mind, all things are possible, and there is perfect freedom. This is the path, therefore, upon which we come and go simultaneously. We return to the crown of the Tree, from whence, aeons ago, we descended; yet at the same time we are prepared to descend once more in order to bring and share life, light, and liberty with all beings. When we have arrived at the Eleventh Path, life is no longer a necessity, but a joyful, free choice. The weariness of the long journey is passed, and unlimited energy permeates the nature of the traveler. What has appeared as work is now play. The Hebrew letter of this path is *Aleph*, meaning "ox." On it, the yoke the traveler receives is indeed easy, and the burden light. It is here one realizes that everything seemingly left behind during the course of the long journey is, in fact, still available. From the physical treasures of Malkuth to the half-human, half-divine beauties of Tiphareth, and even to the ultimate, crowning glory of Kether, all the rewards of the ten heavenly way stations are his. Without attachment to any portion or region of the Tree, he is at one with every leaf and branch, because he has become the essence of the sap that moves through it all. This is the path of truth, laughter, and bliss, where the dewdrop, having slipped into the shining sea, has not become obliterated but freely moves from sea to lake, from river to creek and pond as the embodied power of free and purposeful motion. As one poet and Kabbalist expressed it: "Truth, laughter, light: Life's Holy Fool! Veil rent, lewd madness brings sublime enlightenment."

In antiquity, no celestial attribution was given to this path, but in modern times the planet Uranus is frequently used. The Tarot Trump is the Fool, which is the unnumbered card, having the nonnumber zero as its denominator. A bright, pale shade of yellow is the color; the precious stones are the topaz and the chalcedony. Aspen is the plant, and the eagle as well as humankind are the animals considered appropriate. The magical weapons are the Dagger and the Fan. The perfume is galbanum and the drug, peppermint. The gods of the path are Jupiter, Zeus, and the Valkyries.

Thus we come to the end of our description of the twenty-two highways that join the ten way stations with each other and serve to lead the traveler in an orderly and balanced manner to his destination. The foregoing is intended as a subject of brief but intense study, as a text for a concentrated exercise of intellect and memory, the usefulness of which will reveal itself only in practice. It is to this practice that the following pages are devoted. As stated before, the Kabbalah is not only a subject for study and a source of intellectual stimulation and information. Rather, first and foremost it is a systematic device designed for the purpose of the inward expansion and enhancement of the soul. In the next chapter, we shall turn from description and study to practice, and from thinking to meditation.

# CHAPTER SEVEN

# ᴛʜᴇ
# FOOL'S PILGRIMAGE

The human being is a fool. Shakespeare was right when he said: "What fools we mortals be!" The first card of the greater Arcana, the Fool, pictures man as a carefree youth, striding gaily forth in such a position that his next step may send him over the edge of a cliff. As noted in connection with the Eleventh Path, we are this fool ourselves, divine and immortal souls ready to descend into manifest existence. It is also we ourselves, having descended from Kether to Malkuth, now ascending from earth to the heavens. Of all the Arcana, the Fool manifests the greatest freedom. Although technically attributed to the Eleventh Path, he is in very truth on all paths and in all the sephiroth at the same time, since he is the very life, the nourishing essence, or sap, of the Tree. It is this very freedom that makes him a fool. It is a sad fact of life that men are more afraid of freedom than of anything else, even more than of slavery or death. Being restricted by rules, taboos, and regulations provides the personality—which lacks ego strength—with a feeling of security, without which it would perish like a clam without its shell or a crab without its armor. But the time must come, when, as the Psalmist wrote: "Fears shall be in the way"; that is, when we must grow strong, deriving our fortitude from the inward resources of our soul rather than from the puny constructions of mortal minds and human society. The time must come when we shall be willing to bear the burden of freedom and relinquish the crutches and burdensome armors of tradition, society, church, nation, culture, and family, or any other substitute for the one and only source of all strength, wisdom, and goodness—the union of our individual soul with the divine ground within which it is rooted. The time must come when we recognize and accept ourselves as the fools we are.

What manner of fools are we, indeed? The gods may well have first called us fools when they beheld us in leaving our father's home, going forth into incarnational manifestation. Well it might be that they pointed to our folly of leaving heaven for the hardships of earth. At the other end of the great Jacob's ladder of being, at the base of the Tree of Life in the kingdom of Malkuth, the men of earth, too, are calling us fools. With fortunes to be made, status and fame to be attained, and families to be raised, who but a fool would waste time and strength in the impractical pursuits of philosophy, mysticism, and meditation? The world marches to the music of wealth, power, and pleasure, while some fools listen to a different drummer and walk not in the ways of the world. Whether descending from spirit to matter, or ascending from earth to heaven, we are known as fools. As fools we journey on the many paths of the Tree of Life, but we must not be blind fools. The true mysteries of life have always been regarded as paradoxes by the wise. Thus, much that appears foolishness is in reality but misunderstood wisdom. We can readily change ourselves from blind fools into wise fools, provided we know how.

The wise fool is also known as the jester. The world—both the outer world of men and the inner world of our personality—is a castle filled with intrigue, cares, and strife. Still, in this gloomy fortress there may be a peculiar personage, the castle fool, or jester. He is a person of acknowledged wisdom, even in his folly, and he serves as the foil, the goading force, the thorn in the flesh, the prodder of the masters of the castle. He is the fool, but he is placed in his position to make, at the right time, a "fool" out of the lords and ladies of the manor so that, in their newly acquired folly, they might be wise. It is this role of jester that appertains to the mystic, the seeker after union with God. Within the individual personality, the Higher Self, or mystic fool, forever pokes fun at the worldly goals and methods of the lower ego and prods it on to turn from the ways of the blind fool to those of the wise fool. Similarly, mystics and Gnostics have always been the true salt of the earth, the leaven of every inert society within which they resided. "Where there is no vision, the people perish." A nation or society without individuals who can make contact with the divine world is doomed to failure and downfall.

From ancient days in our culture, April 1 has been known as All Fool's Day. This day is placed in the spring, at the end of the six-month dark cycle of incarnational "folly" that began in the autumn. The time period between the equinox of autumn and that of spring was regarded as the dark or nether half of the year, when the earth is dead, the days short, and the night of expectation long. The fool journeys forth into the lower worlds of earthly darkness for one half of the total cycle of the solar year, while the other half he spends in the bright sunshine of the divine worlds. The lower branches of the Tree of Life, past the middle point of the beauty of Tiphareth, are enveloped in relative darkness; the higher we climb on the branches, however, the sunnier and brighter the world becomes. Thus the lower five sephiroth stand for the dark cycle of the year—namely, the six months of autumn and winter—while the upper five may be symbolized by the sunny six months of spring and summer.

In the springtime of the evolution of the soul, the Fool, like Rip Van Winkle of Washington Irving's American legend, awakens from his aeonial slumber within the tomblike confines of material attachments and walks into the sunlight of spiritual initiation leading to Divine Union. It is on All Fool's Day that the adherents of certain ancient mysteries celebrated this event, when man ceases to be the blind fool of earth and becomes the wise fool of heaven. While he lingered in the lesser worlds of limited consciousness, he was subject to every sort of incertitude, and his once-clear vision was diffracted into distortions of reality, thus making him a blind fool, indeed. Triumphantly rising from the dark half of the cycle, or the dark branches of the Tree into the daylight of divinity, he is now the wise and holy fool who, with a shout of joyous laughter, swings himself into the sunlit branches of the transpersonal worlds when he enters upon the paths above Tiphareth. Still, it is not advisable for us to apply this symbology too literally and to regard the lower worlds as mere vales of sorrow from which we desire to escape. We must remember that the Tree of Life is one and that its lower branches are as necessary as the higher.

To ascend the Tree of Life, to travel on the paths between the heavenly sephirotic cities, is the eternal task of the wise fool. The outer rewards of such endeavors are few indeed; therefore, the traveler is a fool in the eyes of the world. Yet his foolishness is in truth the hallmark of wisdom, for it leads to the greatest treasure any soul can find—the state of being one with life, with love, and with the will that moves through all. The meditational texts that follow are designed to do but one thing: aid the soul in its journeying on the paths of the Tree of Life. This purpose is accomplished when aspirants regard the meditations as signposts reminding them of the origin, destination, and direction of the road upon which they are traveling. In order to permit the meditational texts to penetrate the consciousness of the meditator with sufficient force, it has been necessary to make them brief. Brevity should not be confused with superficiality. The usefulness of a text for the purpose of meditation tends to diminish in proportion to its length. It is also deemed advisable to employ a somewhat poetic style in the wording of the meditations in order to invest them with what Jung called an aura of "numinosity," which is the hallmark of the language of the archetypes. The texts may be read over several times if required, although one reading may be sufficient to produce the desired effect. Those with a facility for memorizing may find it useful to memorize the meditations as they use them, and there is much to be said in favor of this practice. That noble remnant of the mysteries, known as Freemasonry, insists that its rituals and lectures be memorized rather than read, and the better-informed ceremonial magicians entertain similar notions concerning magical texts. At the same time, we must keep in mind that if an excessive amount of psychic energy is required for the task of memorizing, it may deplete the energy reservoir required for the process of meditation itself. Moderation and good judgment are the key.

Of utmost importance to the successful practice of the Kabbalistic meditation here outlined is the use of the images of the appropriate Tarot Arcana. Without the Arcanum in question, the meditational text is well-nigh useless, unless the aspirant can visualize the card in question in every detail. It will therefore be necessary for the meditating person to be aware of three elements simultaneously: (1) the position of the path in question on the Tree of Life, especially in relationship to the two sephiroth which it serves to connect; (2) the appropriate Tarot Arcanum, clearly observed in every detail; and (3) the meditational text, read slowly, recited from memory, or listened to from the accompanying CD, if necessary more than once, until its content has forcefully penetrated the conscious and borderline areas of the psyche.

As a rule, it might be best to repeat the same meditation (the same path) for the duration of one week, having engaged in the exercise once a day at a convenient time, when distractions are least likely to occur. The qualities and the message of the path will thus have sufficient time to become internalized within the emotions and mind. It may also be useful to avail oneself of additional study material regarding the path and the Tarot Arcanum during the week, although this may be considered optional. Utilizing the age-old archetypal cycle, it might be considered advisable to start meditating on a new path every Friday after sundown. There are no requirements regarding posture, gesture, breathing, or diet in connection with these meditations, and it may be important to recall that neither fasting nor overeating is encouraged before meditating. It is advisable to keep one's eyes open for most of the time allocated to the meditational exercise, although they may be closed for a while toward the end. No great importance should be attached to visual imagery arising at such times in the mind, since the Tarot Arcanum and no other is the archetypal image.

Thus the Fool may begin his pilgrimage. Having prepared himself for the journey, having equipped himself with a map of the way stations and highways and informed himself concerning the character and shape of the terrain he will traverse, he may now set his foot on the Royal Road that leads to the crown of the king. Let him go forth as a pilgrim of eternity, homeward bound among the stars!

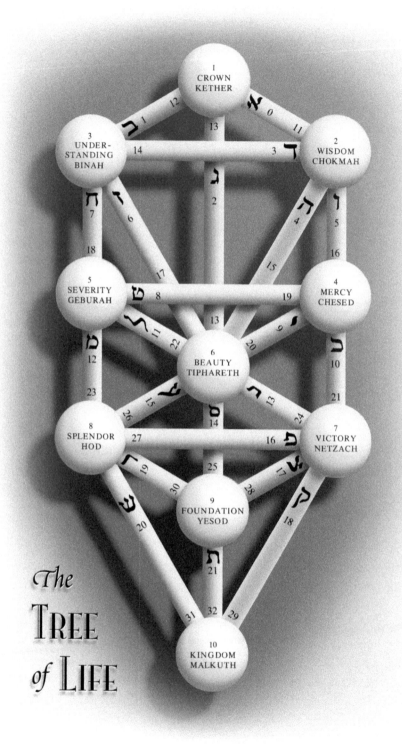

The
TREE
of LIFE

CHAPTER EIGHT

# OBSERVING
# *the*
# SIGNPOSTS

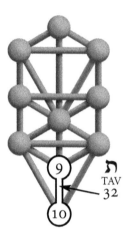

# The World *(Sometimes known as the Universe)*
## The Twenty-First Arcanum

T HE ARCANUM shows a dancer clad only in a scarf, framed by
an oval wreath. In the four corners are the four beasts of Earth,
Water, Fire and Air, the constituents of the manifest world, and the
four functional cornerstones of the human personality; namely,
sensation, feeling, thinking, and intuition. The dancer, who ideally
is a hermaphrodite, holds two wands representing the balance of the
opposites and of involution and evolution. The legs of the dancer
form a cross, while the arms and the torso make up the shape of
a triangle pointing upward, indicating the lower quaternary of the
personality surmounted by the trinity of the higher Self.

# Tav
## The Thirty-Second Path:
## From Malkuth to Yesod

**Keynote:** From imprisonment in form we rise to the consciousness of vital force.

**Motto:** "And ye shall know the truth, and the truth shall make you free."

—JOHN 8:32*

* All biblical references are from the King James Version.

## MEDITATION

*I am not of this world, but a child of the beyond. My home is afar, and I long for the house of my Father. May I rightly commence the journey of return. I consecrate my physical, emotional, mental, and intuitive faculties to the accomplishment of the great work. May the senses of my body, the feelings of my emotions, the thoughts of my mind, and the insights of my intuition serve the great work. There is no part of me that is not of the gods. I resolve to regard all incidents in my life as a portion of the dialogue between my self and the Self. May every part of my being, and every act of my living, be dedicated to the purpose of the return to the home of my Father.*

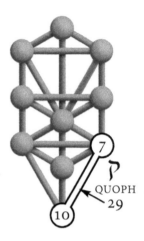

# The Moon
## The Eighteenth Arcanum

T HE MOON, shown in its three phases, looks down upon a nocturnal landscape wherein, from the pool of unconscious emotion, the primitive living form of a crayfish slowly climbs toward distant heights. A wolf and a dog sit beside the road, howling at the moon, representing the wild and the domesticated components of our instinctual nature. The towers of human intellectual and moral defense mechanisms loom on the horizon, to be bypassed on the road to the summit of final attainment. The seeds of divine lifeforce in the form of falling drops, having the shape of the letter Yod, remind us of supernal energy vitalizing the emotional and instinctual self and stirring it into activity.

# Quoph
## The Twenty-Ninth Path:
## From Malkuth to Netzach

**Keynote:** From physical being we rise to the awareness of our emotional nature.

**Motto:** "There is a tide in the affairs of men which, taken at the flood..."

—SHAKESPEARE

## MEDITATION

*May I hear the call from on high! Through the tumult and confusion of the lower worlds, the voice of my Father calls to me from afar. May I never cease to heed this call and rally to the banner of my inward Lord, as the battle of life rages. The Lord of my soul reigns above the waterfloods: He will remove all delusion and confusion from me. I shall stop, listen, and be silent, in order to hear the voice. Louder than the thunder of the falling waters is the still, small voice that resounds from the distant place. I hear thee, O voice above all voices! I heed thee, O call before all calls!*

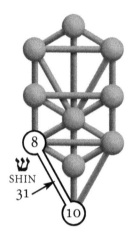

# Judgement
## The Twentieth Arcanum

O UT OF THEIR OPENED SEPULCHERS the dead rise in response
to the clarion call of the angel who, blowing his bannered
trumpet, looms in the heavens. The sepulchers float on the waters
of emotion, while they themselves represent the compartments
and structures of the mind. The angel, surrounded by the blaze of
the solar fire, stands for the Higher Self or Holy Guardian Angel
of the individual, while the awakened human personality is like a
dead man rising to life. Snowy mountain peaks rise on the horizon
beyond the sea, indicating the need for further attainment. The
equal-armed cross on the angelic banner stands for the law of
balance and equilibrium that is ever the supreme signpost of all
progress on the paths of the Tree of Life.

# Shin
## The Thirty-First Path:
## From Malkuth to Hod

**Keynote:** Our total being is renewed when, relinquishing our attachment to physicality, we enter the realm of enlightened mind.

**Motto:** "Marvel not at this: for the hour is coming in ... which all that are in the graves shall hear his voice, And shall come forth."
—JOHN 5:28–9

## *MEDITATION*

*As I hear the clarion call, summoning me to the palace of the King, I shall be renewed within and without. I am a new creature, and all my thoughts, feelings, actions, and insights will be new. I am a child of the divine fire, a spark from the primordial flame. Earth cannot smother me; water cannot drown me. May the breath of my Father fan me into new life and new activity. I am renewed. I resolve to renew myself day by day.*

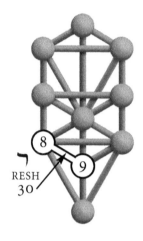

RESH
30

# The Sun
## The Nineteenth Arcanum

A NAKED child rides a white horse and holds a banner aloft. (In other decks, two naked children dance in a circle under the sun.) The many-sided sun smiles down from the sky. Happiness, joy, and victory pervade the entire picture. In the background is a walled garden with golden sunflowers growing in profusion. The conjoining of vital energy with the principle of intellect makes for innocent happiness, like that of happy childhood. Although still a babe in the woods of the Tree of Life, the ascending soul is powerful in its mastery of the horse of emotion and body. The garden of its mind bears fine plants in the image of the vitalized principle of intellect.

ר

# Resh
## The Thirtieth Path:
## From Yesod to Hod

**Keynote:** Joining the principle of vital energy with that of the intellect, the mind becomes filled with great, triumphant force.

**Motto:** "A man's wisdom maketh his face to shine."
—ECCLES. 8:1

## MEDITATION

On the white horse of pure consciousness, I ride into the sun. I am a child of the eternal. I am filled with splendor, light, and power. Nothing can harm me save my own ignorance. Wisdom will make my face shine. I am victorious insight. I shall conquer and prevail. I am a ray of the blazing sun of all universes. I now take my first step toward complete freedom. I shall be free, for I shall dwell in the eternal.

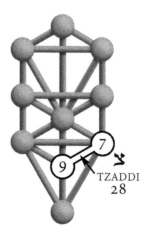

# The Star
## The Seventeenth Arcanum

A BEAUTIFUL, unclad female figure kneels with one knee on the land while her other foot rests on the water of a pool. With two pitchers she pours water on both dry land and into the pool. The meditative soul delves deeply into the waters of the unconscious, into which she pours vital force. She is balanced between the solid and liquid and the physical and emotional poles of being. The guiding star of the Higher Self shines above, reflected in the pool of unconscious emotion. The ibis bird of the enlightened, thinking faculty perches on a tree nearby. The meditative effort brings energy to the conscious self, the earth, where five rivulets of water form, and it stirs the feeling faculty into newer and deeper revelation of its nature.

# Tzaddi
## The Twenty-Eighth Path:
## From Yesod to Netzach

**Keynote:** Vital energy flows into feeling. By energizing emotion, it creates a condition wherein highest guidance becomes accessible, joining the feelings of the personality with Divine Emotion.

**Motto:** "Let there be a firmament in the midst of the waters and let it divide the waters from the waters. And God . . . divided the waters which *were* under the firmament from the waters which *were* above the firmament."

—GEN. 1:6–7

## MEDITATION

*May the never-setting star of my divine and immortal soul ever shine over me. I have a guiding light that is my indwelling God. May I never lose sight of my immortal and divine soul, implanted into my being before the beginning of time. I am within the orbit of God, a planet in the firmament of souls. I am a star as are all other human beings. May my light, in concert with the light of all others, ever shine.*

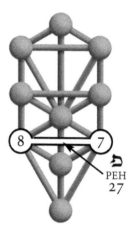

# The Tower *(Sometimes known as the Lightning Struck Tower)*
## The Sixteenth Arcanum

A GAINST the foreboding background of a midnight sky, there looms a strange tower built upon a tall, barren rock. Out of the heavens flashes a bolt of lightning, shearing off the crown at the top of the tower and sending the inhabitants thereof hurtling down. Falling drops of blood or light descend from above in the shape of the Hebrew letter Yod. The building of earthly attachments—of the false structures of mind, emotion, and body—is destroyed by the thunderbolt of the Higher Self. Having built upon the false security of personal and human values, human beings fall from the imagined heights of their own conceit. The Tower of Babel is destroyed because it represents an effort to reach Divinity by purely human means without the relinquishment of personal ambitions and attachments.

# Peh

## The Twenty-Seventh Path:
## From Hod to Netzach

**Keynote:** Mind and Emotion, Form and Life, when joined together generate implacable conflict that can be resolved only by raising consciousness to a level superior to both, thus uniting the eternal thesis and antithesis in a higher synthesis.

**Motto:** "Except the Lord build the house, they labor in vain that build it."

—Ps. 127:1

## *MEDITATION*

*I* am willing to sacrifice all in order to attain to the objective of my great journey. If it is the will of my Father to strike down everything I have built in my life, may He do so and do it swiftly. I shall be free of attachment to anything or anyone. I love all, but I shall be ready to part from all when ordered to do so by the Lord of Fire. I realize that by being attached to the constructs of my personality I shall never be able to soar into the heavens. May all that needs to be destroyed in me be destroyed and blotted out forever; thus I shall rejoice with the voice of thunder and exult with the flash of lightning. So mote it always be.

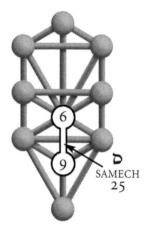

SAMECH
25

# Temperance
## The Fourteenth Arcanum

A MAJESTIC winged angel identified by some authorities as Michael, archangel of the element of fire, stands with one foot on the earth and the other in the water. He pours an essence from one cup into another, indicating the transfer of vital forces from one level to another. Above the distant peaks the sun is rising, and a brilliant path leads in its direction. Balance, serenity, and fiery strength characterize the entire picture, indicating the poised, purposefully directed, well-proportioned energy required for the reaching of supernal states of consciousness. The quality of adaptation, equilibrium, and coordination symbolized are described by the name "Temperance."

84

# Samech
## The Twenty-Fifth Path:
## From Yesod to Tiphareth

**Keynote:** Properly balanced between intellect and feeling, the soul calls on the vital force to propel it into the region of consciousness where divine illumination occurs.

**Motto:** "An angel bendeth o'er thee, And bears thee to the stand; And, filled with joy, before thee, Thou seest the Promised Land."
—NOVALIS (FRIEDRICH VON HARDENBERG)

## MEDITATION

*T*hrough the central gate of balanced being, I enter into the palace of my glorious King. I call upon my faithful helpers, courage and sincerity, to aid my passage through the gates of gold. Humbly I bow my knees before the beauty of Him who reigns from the center of my being. I contemplate the glorious beauty of the one who resides at the heart of all creatures. May my mind be aware of His magnificence and my heart be irradiated by His love. I will direct the holy fire within my body and soul, so that the arrow of my will may be aimed at the supreme goal. The arrow flies into the heart of the all! May the arrow and its target remain forever united in beauty and love.

85

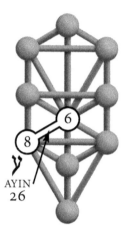

# The Devil
## The Fifteenth Arcanum

A GIGANTIC devil-figure with a goat's head, bat wings, human torso, shaggy legs, and bird feet sits on a half-cube. His right hand is raised in a gesture of saturnine rejection against the heavens, while his left hand holds the inverted torch of destruction. Two human figures, one male, the other female, possessing horns and tails, are chained to the seat of the devil, their chains being loose so as to allow for their escape. The lower mind—which, like the mountain goat, scales the pinnacles of the material world—holds the soul in bondage until, with determination, we slip out of its shackles. Although outwardly formidable, the goat of the world has no real power to keep man from his heavenly destiny. By ceasing to yield to demonic illusion, we begin to see worldly attachments and cares as ridiculous, and we laugh the laughter of the gods!

# Ayin
## The Twenty-Sixth Path:
## From Hod to Tiphareth

**Keynote:** From consciousness of the world we move to the wisdom of God. The beauty and splendor of divine illumination beckon to us from the summit of equipoise, and we free ourselves from delusion in order to reach it.

**Motto:** "Canst thou, poor Devil, give me whatsoever? When was a human soul, in its supreme endeavour, E'r understood by such as thou?"

—GOETHE, *Faust*, part 1

## MEDITATION

*From the depths of limitation, I call to thee, O beauty ineffable! Shine upon my path, thou midnight sun of beauty and love! I shall endure the darkness, and I shall dwell in the dungeon of outer dark places, if only I know that thy day is approaching. O never-setting sun of my soul, I call upon thy radiant beauty. Turn my ignorance into wisdom and my passions into love for thee. For it is thou whom I have loved throughout the aeons, and it is thou whom I seek in every place. Give me lightness of heart so that I may loosen my chains of servitude and fly into thine arms, my hope, my lover, and sole liberator!*

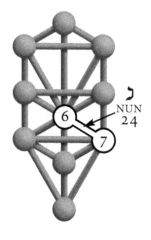

# Death
## The Thirteenth Arcanum

AN AMORED, mounted skeleton rides over a field, where people of various stations in life are reduced to the common condition of lifelessness. In some decks the traditional grim-reaper skeleton is used for the same purpose. A square banner bearing a five-petaled rose flies overhead, showing the perennial victorious combining of the four- and five-fold constituent elements of the cosmos. The river of life flows by peacefully, while on the horizon, between the two columns, or towers, the rising divine sun shines from its position of balance. The total impression created by this Arcanum is one of change and renewal rather than of irrevocable destruction.

# Nun
## The Twenty-Fourth Path:
## From Netzach to Tiphareth

**Keynote:** Only the empty cup can be filled. If our hearts are to be irradiated with Divine Love, all human loves and attachments must pass away. The many must die in order to make way for the One.

**Motto:** "O death, where *is* thy sting? O grave, where *is* thy victory?"
—1 COR. 15:55

## MEDITATION

*All endings are but beginnings in thee, O my glorious King, the central sun! May I remember it is in dying that I shall awaken to life eternal and to light sublime. May the darkness be brought to death in me so that the light may shine. The night is passing as the day approaches. That which I have sown in the outer world must die so that, by dying, it may awaken to new life in the world of my true soul. That which I have sown is not quickened except it dies. I shall welcome the destruction of all obstacles and unregenerate forces within my nature, so that I may be reconstructed in God!*

89

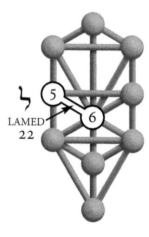

# Justice
## The Eleventh Arcanum

THE FIGURE of Justice is seated in a position of balance between the two pillars of the polar opposites. She is Divine Justice, having her eyes unveiled, rather than human justice, which is blind. Her sword is lifted as a symbol of her potential severity. In her left hand, she holds the scales of balanced judgment. To the open eyes of this figure, all things are revealed, and the sword of Karma in her right hand will inevitably smite all imperfection and selfishness. Past and present are both weighed in the golden scales, and if the karmic weight is in balance, progress is assured for the pilgrim. Impartial, unbending, yet ultimately beneficent is the image conveyed by this Arcanum.

ל

# Lamed
## The Twenty-Second Path:
## From Tiphareth to Geburah

**Keynote:** From the way station of balanced beauty, we move to the principle of severity, and while so doing the karmic forces of purification subject us to a thorough process of judgment.

**Motto:** "Be not deceived; God is not mocked: for whatsoever a man soweth, that shall he also reap."

—GAL. 6:7

## MEDITATION

*I ask for clarity of judgment, so that I may give a clear account of my motives and actions. As I proceed on the path from manhood to godhead, I must be aware of all my motives and intentions. I shall weigh the results of the law of causation, and I shall walk within the law. Though I have seen the royal beauty and felt the love of the King, I am not above the law. Yea, lest I abide within the law, all my efforts will come to naught. The King is good, but He is also just. May I follow His command, and the sword of His justice will defend and uphold me unto the glorious end.*

91

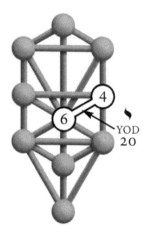

# The Hermit
## The Ninth Arcanum

A TOP a snowy mountain peak, in solitary splendor, a hooded and robed hermit stands holding the lamp of the spirit and leaning upon the staff of intuition. He is garbed in the mantle of discretion and unobtrusively shows the way to all who dare to follow him. He walks the path of the flight of the alone to the alone, but upon his adeptic example depend countless aspirants to initiation into the mysteries of the spirit. He is no longer a man of the world, but has not yet joined the company of the gods. Thus his loneliness is vast beyond belief and glorious beyond all imagination.

# Yod
## The Twentieth Path:
## From Tiphareth to Chesed

**Keynote:** From human love, sacrificed upon the altar of beauty, we proceed to all-sustaining Divine Love, thereby undergoing the loneliness of one who sacrificed all he was, without having yet become what he shall be.

**Motto:** "Stand alone and isolated, because nothing that is embodied, nothing that is conscious of separation, nothing that is out of the Eternal, can aid you."
—MABEL COLLINS, *Light on the Path*

## MEDITATION

*I n the lonely hour of my soul, thou comest to my chamber, O beauty and love sublime. I lean upon the rod and staff of my insight, and though I walk through the valley of solitude and scale the summits of loneliness, I know that my lover awaits on the mountaintop, from whence ever cometh my help. In the midst of the turmoil of living, I am but a lonely wanderer seeking my love. A pilgrim of eternity am I, homeward bound among the stars.*

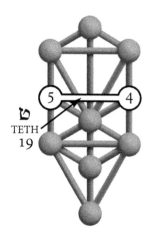

# Strength
## The Eighth Arcanum

A FEMALE figure, garlanded with flowers and surmounted by the sign of infinity, holds in her hands the muzzle of a lion, whose mouth she is in the process of either closing or opening. The woman is robed in the white of purity and pure spiritual force, while the lion is red, indicating passion and emotional energy. The power exercised by the woman over the beast is evidently of a spiritual character rather than brute strength, and her dominion over it appears to be a gentle one. Eternity bestows on her a strength that is not of this world.

# Teth

## The Nineteenth Path:
## From Geburah to Chesed

**Keynote:** The balancing or connecting of mercy and severity is accomplished when the beast within is tamed and its power turned to the service of the purposes of the spirit.

**Motto:** "O Lion and O Serpent that destroy the destroyer, be mighty among us!"

— from a Gnostic Mass

## Meditation

*As I join justice with love in my life, I know that I require fortitude to proceed on my journey. In order to face the severity of the spirit, I must gird my loins with strength ineffable and great. Gently I will tame the great beast that dwells in my nature, recognizing that it too is my friend. The claws of the lion will be my helpers on the path: They will terrify my enemies and open the gates before me. I will learn the paths of the power of the serpent within my passions so that I may enlist its aid. With the aid of the lion and the serpent, I shall fear no evil and shall not be troubled by any obstacle. Victorious strength is mine when I have tamed the lion of power.*

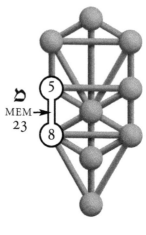

ל
MEM→
23

# The Hanged Man
## The Twelfth Arcanum

A MAN is suspended by one foot from a T-shaped tree. His arms, folded behind his back, together with his head, form a triangle that is pointed upward; while his right leg crossed behind his left leg forms a triangle with its point downward. He is thus rooted in heaven and appears to exist in a condition that is unnatural and contrary to the world. The opposites are balanced in his being, and, in spite of his seemingly uncomfortable position, he is in a state of peace and serenity, which manifests in the saintly halo around his head.

# Mem
## The Twenty-Third Path:
## From Hod to Geburah

**Keynote:** From the sphere of thinking we ascend to the principle of merciless, unbending leadership. In order to accomplish this ascent, we subject our concepts and precepts to a transvaluation and a reordering of inward priorities.

**Motto:** "Walk in all things contrary to the world."
—JACOB BOEHME

## MEDITATION

On the cross that hangs betwixt heaven and earth, I am suspended in utter balance. By sacrificing all that I have been, I shall inherit the state of my future being. Although my head is in the lower worlds, my eye is directed to the luminaries of the heavens. I am a tree of life, rooted in the divine soil. My roots reach into the heart of God, and my crown is upon the earth. I am the manifest glory, suspended between the extremities of high and low, and I shall be balanced, calm, and victorious in the midst of sacrifice and reversal. Those of little wisdom will think me a fool who walks not in their ways, but I know the hidden design of the one who sent me. I float upon the waters of the great sea, and I am safe from the storm. In me the mystery that is suspended in the cosmos shall be fulfilled.

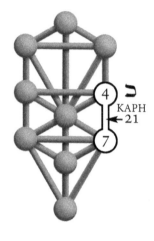

# The Wheel of Fortune
## The Tenth Arcanum

S USPENDED IN SPACE, and surrounded by the four symbolic
beasts of the elements representing the psychological functions
of sensation, emotion, thinking, and intuition, the Wheel (*Rota*) of
Fortune turns. Descending on the arc of generation we see a serpent, while ascending in regeneration we find the jackal-headed figure of Anubis, god of enlightened mentality. The principle of balance and equilibrium rules the wheel in the shape of a sphinx armed
with a sword. The three circles constituting the wheel indicate the
triune, Higher Self, composed of will, love, and creative ideation.
The alchemical symbols making up the spokes of the wheel indicate
the transmutation of the soul within the whirling process of change.

# Kaph
## The Twenty–First Path:
## From Netzach to Chesed

**Keynote:** Progressing from the lesser fortune of human emotion to the greater fortune of Divine Benevolence, we may deem ourselves fortunate indeed, but only if we have learned to reconcile and integrate the four-fold functions of our personality, and only if we are and continue to remain ruled by perfect balance.

**Motto:** "Behold . . . his reward *is* with him, and his work before him. . . . Who hath measured the waters in the hollow of his hand, and meted out heaven with the span." —ISA. 40: 10, 12

## *MEDITATION*

*I receive the reward of my labors. The wheel of the law will turn in my favor, and I shall rule the four corners of my internal being. May I remember that I am called to mastery over my self and not to mastery over the goods of the world. My gold shall be in the noonday sun of love, and my silver in the midnight moon of knowledge. I am fortunate indeed to have been led to walk with the light of the holy ones and in the company of the just. My existence extends from the mountaintop of heaven to the depths of hell, and I am master of all. The wheel turns for good: May I be willing and capable to act as a spoke in the great wheel that ever moves for beauty, goodness, and truth. Turn, wheel of the holy law, so that the great body of God may advance toward the goal of its own fulfillment! I greet thee, O royal chariot wheel of the kingdom of righteousness, and I shall serve thee unto the glorious end.*

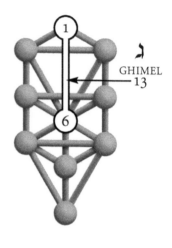

GHIMEL
—13

# The High Priestess
## The Second Arcanum

BETWEEN the two pillars of light and darkness, or mercy and severity, seated in the position of central balance, we find the High Priestess. On her head she wears the symbol of the full moon, and under her feet we find the image of the lunar crescent. Equilibrium is again indicated by the equal-armed solar cross on her breast, while from her cloak she draws the book of the sacred law. She is the intuitively feminine virginal guardian of the temple of the mysteries, the enigmatic mistress of the night, whose blue cloak covers and reveals the nature of sacred nocturnal journeys. Though she is a virgin, the pomegranates and palms on the temple veil behind her indicate the operation of the energies of the male and female polarities.

# Ghimel
## The Thirteenth Path:
## From Tiphareth to Kether

**Keynote:** On the central column, or the straight path of the arrow, we proceed from the first point of contact between the human and divine worlds to the highest crown of the godhead on a perilous midnight journey, precariously balanced on the back of the camel.

**Motto:** "The Indescribable, Here it is done; The Woman-soul leadeth us Upward and on!"

—GOETHE, Faust, part 2

## ⲘEDITATION

On the ship of the desert I ride across the vast wasteland of the soul. O thou silvery moon, my guide and light, shine on my path! All ye stars and luminaries of the heavens, guide me through the perils of the great journey, so that I may arrive at the supreme crown of my being and enter the ineffable splendor of the last chamber of the palace! The road to the great crown of final victory leads through the peril of the abyss, where the quicksand of temptation may destroy me. Only balance can save me from plunging into the pit. Therefore, I will invoke into my personality the power of balance; poised between the light and dark pillars of my being, serenely and firmly I shall hasten to the mysterious place where the voiceless voice of the beloved calls to me day and night.

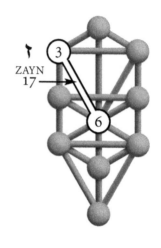

ZAYN
17

# The Lovers
## The Sixth Arcanum

A NUDE MALE AND FEMALE figure stand in an open field, while an angel hovers overhead. The man stands for the animus (masculine soul-component), while the woman represents the anima (female soul-component) within the individual. The two must be reconciled and united in a fitting manner, and this work is accomplished through angelic guidance. Behind the woman is the tree of the knowledge of good and evil, symbolic of living nature (eros), while behind the man is a tree bearing flames, symbolic of the intellectual-spiritual nature (logos). A high mountain looms in the background, indicating further summits the pair is to climb together. The noonday sun of divine illumination shines overhead, sustaining human and angelic nature alike.

# Zayn
## The Seventeenth Path:
## From Tiphareth to Binah

**Keynote:** From a position of balanced illumination, consciousness now travels to the restrictive and often sorrowful state of profound understanding. Such an experience can best be faced if the inner opposites of the soul are completely reconciled and constant guidance from the Higher Self (Holy Guardian Angel) is available.

**Motto:** "When you make the male and the female into a single one, so that the male will not be male and the female not be female . . . then shall you enter the Kingdom."
—THE GOSPEL OF THOMAS, LOGION 22

## *MEDITATION*

*A*s I ascend into the regions of my true nature, I must renounce all that does not pertain to the supernal worlds. May I have the judgment and discernment to make the right choice. May my mind be enlightened by angelic guidance and divine illumination so that I may choose between the important and the unimportant, even the supreme good and the lesser good. The judgment of supernal conscience will smite me if my choice is not right. Come, enlightening presence of my indwelling guardian, and show me the way to the holy wedding chamber of the soul, where I shall wed the counterpart of my being. Only by uniting myself in mystic marriage with my twin shall I be found whole and fit to enter the kingdom. Love and wisdom will make me worthy to pass the gates of judgment and permit me to enter the empire of boundless light.

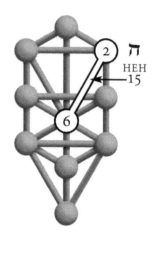

ה
HEH
—15

# The Emperor
## The Fourth Arcanum

COMMANDING AND REGAL, the Emperor sits on his rock-hewn throne, which is decorated with the emblems of Aries, indicating fiery strength. The feminine power of love and the male force of life-giving potency are balanced in his hands as orb and scepter. Seated on a mountain of barren rock, he rules over the world of matter and has mastered the strength to rise above it. Order, virility, paternity, and the lawful regulation of life are embodied in this Arcanum of the kingly man who becomes a reigning god by transmuting earthly power into the spiritual power of unlimited love.

# Heh
## The Fifteenth Path:
## From Tiphareth to Chokmah

**Keynote:** The harmonious condition of enlightenment allows the soul to travel to the source of Divine Love, which is the inseminating father principle of all creation. It is thus that we gain a window into eternity and behold our Father who is in heaven.

**Motto:** "The highest virtue, like a halo-zone, circles the Emperor's head; and he alone is worthy validly to exercise it."

—GOETHE, *Faust*, part 2

## MEDITATION

*I am a man among men. A child of earth am I; yet in me burns the fire of the highest heavens. May the fire of love and goodness so purify the earthborn nature of my personal self that I may be found worthy to enter the sanctuary of the temple of true love. Only the pure in heart can truly love. Let there be no self in my love. Let the beloved be all, and self be naught. O love, that drawest forth the sparks of holiness from the earth, lead me to the rose upon the cross of gold! O love, that art the lifeblood of the universe and the sustainer of my soul, give me strength to ascend unto thee! From the shadows lead me into thy compassionate radiance!*

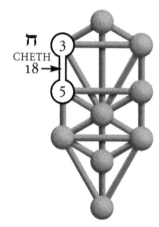

ה
CHETH
18 →
3
5

# The Chariot
## The Seventh Arcanum

A CROWNED, armored, royal warrior rides in a war chariot drawn by one light and one dark colored sphinx, depicting the opposites of manifest existence. The wand of will in his hands tames the beasts of the opposites. A canopy of stars over his head, and lunar crescents on his shoulders, indicate that he knows and uses the power of celestial influences. The chariot he drives has four corners, indicating the four-fold lesser human self; behind him, the silhouette of a walled city shows that he has left behind the world of form in order to conquer the unchartered regions of formless divine power. Unyielding, irreversible power radiates from this Arcanum, depicting the soul bent on conquering the supernal kingdom.

# Cheth
## The Eighteenth Path:
## From Geburah to Binah

**Keynote:** This path is one of extreme power, since it connects two severe principles. Lest we soften our experiences of relentless power on this path, we shall be tempted to become infatuated with power and shall be prone to misuse it. It is therefore important at this point to be conscious of our need to be unselfish, compassionate, and utterly dedicated to the Almighty Will that fulfills itself in us.

**Motto:** "Take unto you the whole armor of God, that ye may be able to withstand in the evil day, and having done all, to stand."
—EPH. 6:13

## MEDITATION

*T*he supreme will commands me to go forth and do battle for the divine king. I am a warrior of the heavens, combating the darkness of earth. Conqueror of the elements and controller of universal forces am I, but the sharpness of my understanding and the severity of my judgment must be curbed by kindness and love. Let truth be my sword and compassion my shield, so that I may conquer through divine balance. I, the warrior of the light, command the darkness to recede, so that all travelers may pass safely into the Promised Land. My personality is the expression of the supreme will: My mind is the embodiment of the power of the one who sent me.

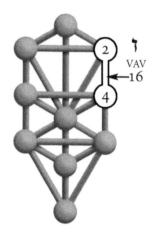

# The Hierophant
## The Fifth Arcanum

CLAD in the eucharistic vestments of a supreme pontiff and seated upon a throne between the two pillars of the opposites, the hierophant raises his right hand in high priestly benediction, while his left hand holds the patriarchal cross of the four elements. The crossed keys of the double kingdom of heaven and earth, the higher and lower selves of man, adorn the platform of the hierophant's throne, while two tonsured priests kneel before him, symbolizing the intellectual and the desirous nature of man, both being dedicated, in this instance, to the service of divine love and grace.

# Vav

## The Sixteenth Path:
## From Chesed to Chokmah

**Keynote:** Uniting the principles of love and wisdom, this path denotes the high initiation of Divine Love, or authentic compassion, which makes it incumbent upon the initiate to be an impersonal, all-beneficent administrator of supernal grace and power, a builder of a bridge between God and man.

**Motto:** "Priest and victim, whom of old type and prophesy foretold, thee incarnate we behold."
—A Catholic Litany of Solemn Benediction

## MEDITATION

*In the temple of my soul, I find the throne of the priest of love and wisdom. Clothed with the gold of wisdom and flaming with the scarlet fire of love, he raises his benevolent hand in perpetual benediction over me. O thou who blessest without ceasing and absolvest without recrimination, humbly I approach thy seat of mercy and ask for thy wisdom! Thou who art priest and king, who art both lover and teacher, thou art my blessing perpetual and enlightenment sublime! I prostrate myself before thy power. I permit the fire of thy love and the stream of thy wisdom to enter my being. Thou revealer of the mysteries profound and bestower of the powers of love, be with me today and forever, O high priest of my soul!*

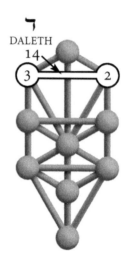

# The Empress
## The Third Arcanum

CROWNED with a diadem of stars, and holding a scepter surmounted by a globe, a majestic, robed woman is seated in blooming, growing nature. On her heart-shaped shield, the emblem of Venus is emblazoned. Surrounding her are numerous plants associated with mother goddesses, as are many of her adornments. Universal fecundity and matronal benevolence radiate from this Arcanum, which is designed to symbolize the doorway of the double birth of the soul. On the initial pathway, it has to do with generation, the birth of things, beings, and ideas; while on the pathway of return, it has to do with regeneration, the birth of the divinity out of the womb of humanity. For this reason, in some Tarot decks, the Empress is portrayed as pregnant.

ד

# Daleth
## The Fourteenth Path:
## From Binah to Chokmah

**Keynote:** Wisdom, our Supernal Father, and Understanding, our Supernal Mother, are united by a power that is the ultimate root of all love, affection, and desire for union. The binaries of anima and animus attain to their ultimate union, and transubstantiated humanity is born as true divinity.

**Motto:** "And there appeared a great wonder in heaven; a woman clothed with the sun, and the moon under her feet, and upon her head a crown of twelve stars: And she being with child cried, travailing in birth ..." —REV. 12:1-2

## *MEDITATION*

*T*he holy doorway leads from life to life: from father to mother and from mother to father. Supreme balance joins love and truth in my heart. Crowned with the stars of truth and shielded by the emblems of the rulership of love, I shall be enthroned serenely in the garden of my triumphant soul. The seeds sown on earth shall grow and flower in the fields of the heavens. The harvest of love has come; let me rejoice and give thanks! Sown in corruption and confusion, the seed of love and truth has grown into the fullness of an incorruptible state, where it shall prosper eternally. O, holy queen of eternal summer, I implore thee to reign in my heart forever!

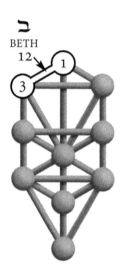

# The Magician
## The First Arcanum

H OLDING his wand aloft in his right hand and pointing with his left to the ground, which is covered with flowers, the Magician stands before a table, upon which the Pentacle, Cup, Sword, and Wand, symbols of the four elements, or four functions of the lesser self, are laid. Above his head is the sign of infinity, and his robes, as well as the vegetation, are characterized by the dual aspect of unmanifest purity and the operative cosmic power of the one eternal spirit. As the lesser being is properly reordered on the table of life, the Magician may freely draw involving power from above and channel evolving life from below toward its supernal destination.

# Beth
## The Twelfth Path:
## From Binah to Kether

**Keynote:** From the source of form to the essence of formlessness, the soul travels while conjoining the power of becoming with the nature of being. As understanding reaches into the heart of divinity, supreme illumination and boundless power become the experience of the soul.

**Motto:** "Hark . . . from the deep, unfathomable vortex of that golden light in which the Victor bathes, all nature's wordless voice in thousand tones ariseth to proclaim: *Joy unto Ye, O men of Myalba* [Earth]. *A Pilgrim hath returned back 'from the other shore.' A new Arhan* [liberated one] *is born. Peace to all Beings.*"
—H. P. BLAVATSKY, *The Voice of the Silence*

## MEDITATION

*Source of power, Father of wisdom, fountain of the stream of life, I pay homage to thee! Thou art the wielder of the wand of power, the wise one, who ordereth the combinations of the elements of my being: be my guide! I need to be transformed, to be changed. From a child of darkness I want to be changed into a being of light. From a creature of impulse, I must become a being of enlightened will. Transform me, O magical lord of my soul! Bring into my personality the flash of divine lightning, so that I may awaken to the consciousness of my authentic nature. I was a man; now I shall be a god. I was of the earth; now I join the stars. Hail to thee, sun of the firmament of my soul! I am thy light, I am thy love, thy wisdom and thy power!*

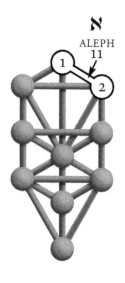

ALEPH
11

# The Fool
## The Zero Arcanum

O N THE SUNLIT height of a summit striding toward a precipice, a youthful figure appears in a graceful, dance-like pose. The white rose of purity is in one hand; with the other he holds a staff with the bag of the traveler, engaged in the eternal journey of the spirit. His eyes are fixed upon the heavens, and at his heels a small dog, symbol of the instincts, gallops along joyously. The sun behind him is rising, for the divine sun never can reach its zenith, but ascends forever. The eternal traveler, who freely roams over all regions of being, prepared and ready for any task, be it liberation or limitation, is regarded a fool, but is master over the All.

# Aleph
## The Eleventh Path:
## From Chokmah to Kether

**Keynote:** The pure essence of the soul takes the last step, completing the conscious linking of all aspects of the supernal states of divinity. It having become one with all, its future is the future of a being whose growth and splendor have no limit.

**Motto:** "I went from God to God, until they cried from me in me—
'O Thou I!' "

—Abu Yazid al-Bistami

## MEDITATION

*The sublime purity of ineffable essence is present within my being. I recognize myself as an essence without form, without qualities and limitations. I am all in all. I am no thing, but I am present in all things. I am the terminal point of all and the first origination of beginning. I was and was not; I am and am not; I shall be, yet I am utterly without a future. I am a circle with its center everywhere and circumference nowhere. Childlike and ancient, young and old, new and aged am I. Purer than the snow, more radiant than the sun, smaller than the smallest atom, greater than the vastness of space: all these I am. I am the all and the naught: I am free. So I am, and was, and shall be, within being and in nonbeing, within time and out of time, ever and never. Amen.*

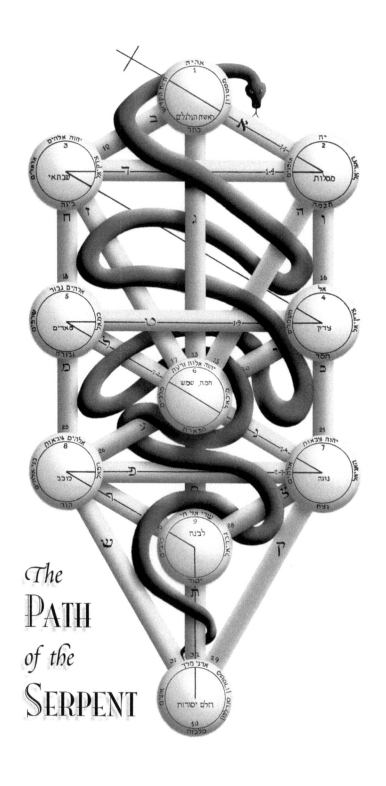

The PATH of the SERPENT

CHAPTER NINE

# *The* ROAD
# GOES EVER ON

One of the most meaningful representations of the Tree of Life shows the Tree with a serpent winding along each path in such a manner that all the twenty-two paths are touched, and thus bound together, by the serpent of wisdom. The tail of the serpent is located where the Thirty-second Path begins at Malkuth, and its head rests upon the Eleventh Path, connecting Kether and Chokmah. Frequently applied to this diagram is the statement from a venerable Kabbalistic work, the *Old Commentary*: "Let the disciple seize hold of the tail of the serpent of wisdom, and having with firmness grasped it, let him follow it into the deepest center of the Hall of Wisdom." The position of the head of the serpent on the mysterious Eleventh Path, the path of the Fool in terms of the Tarot, suggests the possibility that, having climbed to the crown of the Tree of Life, the serpent may not remain there, but may commence to slither down through the branches in order to reach the firm ground of Malkuth once more.

In the foregoing chapters we have, by way of analogy, likened the process of guided meditation on the Tarot Trumps to a journey. It may be useful to call to mind at this point that analogies can at best but attempt to illustrate a truth—to put a point across, as it were—but that they ought not to be taken too literally. Like all metaphors and analogies, the idea of a journey, portraying the successive expansive experiences of consciousness on the paths of the Tree, has some grave shortcomings. Implicit in our ordinary concept of a journey is that it is undertaken in order to reach a particular destination and ends when we arrive at the goal. Most myths of the journey are based on just this idea. The Bible story conceives of the exodus of the chosen people from Egypt as a one-way trip to the Promised Land, and so do many similar tales. Instructive as they are, there is also something very wrong with these accounts.

The experience of living teaches us that life has no static objective. Humanity and nature are forever becoming, but never fully become. We grow, not in order to arrive at a fixed level of growth, but because growth is essential to our own well-being. When we move from one area of experience to another, we remain as we have always been—a center of consciousness moving through an ever-changing panorama of activity and environment. To accept that life is purposeful and meaningful does not inevitably lead to the conclusion that its objective is any particular condition or place. Indeed, the true reason for the journey may well be the journey itself.

Are we then to assume we are enmeshed in an interminable process that never attains to its own fulfillment? Are we destined, or, more correctly, doomed to travel on the paths of the Tree of Life eternally, without any hope of liberation from the constantly recurring chain of attainment? Kabbalistic teaching affirms the reality of an ultimate state of being from which all ideas, creatures, and things come, in which they exist and to which they finally return. The substance of this absolute existence defies and transcends definition, although an occasional intimation of its nature may be received from suggestive mystical phrases. Among the latter, one particular statement comes to mind because of its association with the faith that, if not necessarily the originator, at least served as the long-time custodian of the Kabbalah. This is the great symbolic cry of the wandering sons of Jacob, which strangely reverberates through the halls of the ages: "Hear O Israel, the Lord our God, the Lord is One!" The unitary nature of the indefinable, immeasurable, ultimate essence that, being all in all, pours itself into the sephirotic vessels and becomes the many represents the key to the dilemma under consideration. Unity and multiplicity, totality and incompleteness, perfection and imperfection are not polar opposites, separate from and irreconcilable with each other, but expressions of the same thing, sides of the same coin.

The grand Kabbalistic image of the divinely emanated structural pattern of the all, known as the Tree of Life, may be regarded as the very embodiment of the mystic union of unity and diversity or, for that matter, the unity of all opposites. The Tree is one, but ten are its spheres of power, and twenty-two the ways between these spheres. Light and dark, munificence and restriction, anabolism and katabolism, form and life, are all represented in a balanced, harmonious arrangement in a superbly functioning working order on the design of the Tree. When contemplating the nature of what we called the journey from the base of the Tree to its crown, it is essential that we continue to adhere to the vision of this unity, lest we be deceived by the multiplicity and consequently draw the wrong conclusions from a potentially helpful and meaningful analogy.

Religious-philosophical thought has always been characterized by two tendencies for looking at the problem of the availability of ultimate consciousness. One tends to emphasize the remoteness of ultimate Being, while the other affirms its presence in the here and now. The former is known as the "doctrine of transcendence" and the latter, as the "doctrine of immanence." The enlightened vision of authentic mystics has recognized both of these doctrines as valid and complementary. Humanity is both far from and near to God at the same time. The explanation for this seeming paradox is that we are not divided from the goal of union with God by time and place but by limitations within ourselves. One of the most profound mystic truths of being is embodied in the axiom of the Kabbalah: "Kether is in Malkuth!" If Malkuth is envisioned as the starting point of the journey, and Kether its final goal, we must be aware that there is no first and last way station in the ordinary sense, and that, in reality, the end and the beginning are one. If Kether is remote from Malkuth, it is so not because it is far removed in time and space, but because consciousness in Malkuth has difficulties in recognizing Kether's presence. Thus Kabbalism affirms the immediate availability of complete spiritual experience, and it bases this affirmation on the unity of the Tree, which is a manifestation of the unity of God.

If it appears to us that the goal of the journey is far off, it is because we are unable to recognize that it is closer than breathing and nearer than hands and feet. The long journey home is long because most people cannot rapidly attain detachment from the illusion of limitation they have created in their own minds. Our progress on the paths of the Tree of Life is a growth toward an experience of totality, not a movement from one condition to another. The objective is not to reach Kether, but to arrive at the conscious realization of our identity with the entire Tree. The serpent of wisdom, upon having completed its aeonial task of climbing the Tree, stretches its body over the entire height of the Tree; its tail is on earth and its head above the highest heavens. From these considerations, it also follows that, regardless of the exercises in which we engage in order to reach the crown of the Tree, we cannot do so in order to remain there. As we mentioned in a previous chapter in connection with the figure of the Fool, the greatest treasure we are apt to discover at the crown of the Tree of Life is freedom. This freedom is of a positive character. We become free to travel up and down the great Tree without restriction, very much as if we had become its sap, its life-giving essence. All religions affirm in some manner that it is humankind's ultimate destiny to become one with the Divine Power that governs and sustains creation and its creatures. The philosophy of the Kabbalah, with its teachings concerning our ability to climb the Tree of Life, represents but one particular application of this universal contention.

Once we have come to recognize that inward union with the true source of our being is not a far off, final goal, but a potentially available experience in the present, we shall be less apt to be disappointed by the results of our meditational exercises, including those described in the previous chapters. We may climb the Tree many times, over and over again, and each time we may find a somewhat different, and possibly deeper, quality of experience emerging in the course of our meditations. We shall have no eagerness to progress in haste from one path—and one card—to another, but will relish the subtleties of each individual meditation without relating it to any experience in the past or future. Thus by stages and degrees, each illuminating and rewarding in itself, we may continue to assimilate the experiences of the paths and spheres of the Tree of Life and gradually become increasingly united with its totality in our inner being. The journey is an inward one, and, once it is understood as such, it becomes increasingly a quiet and pleasant road, filled with wonder and the exhilaration of ever-new and inspiring experiences. As drops and rivulets of water mingle to form large rivers that flow into the ocean, so individual travelers on the paths of the Tree of Life will find that their countless inner experiences will mingle and return to the ocean of consciousness, thereby enriching their life.

Some psychological insights may also be helpful here. The unconscious is forever revealing itself through the release of archetypal symbols that rise to the surface of our conscious awareness. As we continue to engage the totality of our conscious and unconscious being in the process of a discipline of internal realization, the symbols will enter our field of vision with ever-greater regularity and increasing power. Detachment from the extroverted pursuits of unenlightened living, and an increasing liveliness of the unconscious archetypes, will not result in neurosis. Quite to the contrary, it will establish a safety valve for the forces below the threshold of consciousness, so that by expressing themselves in a constructive manner, they will lose their menacing potential. Still, meditation on the paths of the Tree is not a form of psychotherapy, at least not in any accepted sense of that word. On the other hand, the mystical experiences connected with working the paths can take on a pathological character, but only if ulterior motives of some kind have been permitted to intrude themselves into the quest for reality. Meditation, prayer, and magic as means of attaining a state of superiority are usually but personal ambition masquerading under the veil of religion. Those who seek wisdom because they desire to be wise leave their psychic structure wide-open to the intrusion of power complexes and related unsavory denizens of the unconscious. Neither are reported experiences of mystic illumination in themselves qualified to present a guarantee of their own genuineness. People are capable of inner experiences of great power and of impressive associations that are, nevertheless, without any essential validity. When the conduct of an allegedly illumined person exhibits few if any of the authentic indications of enlightenment, we may be assured that person's experience belongs to the category of the psychopathological instead of the mystical. The most important single factor in the entire field of the search and striving for insight and wisdom is the motive moving the seeker. Students of the Kabbalah, the Tarot, or any other discipline of inner realization must answer for themselves with complete sincerity and absolute honesty the question, "Why do I wish to develop my latent inner potential?" Only through continued examination of their motives and an alert observation of their reactions to the circumstances of their own life can aspirants understand the true character of the forces that compel or impel their conduct. The psychological balance and ultimate sanity of those practicing some sort of spiritual discipline is almost inevitably dependent on their motives, which must be lacking in the sense of ego. At no time should the seeker after the inner light become interested in *his* light, *his* illumination, *his* own power; for by so doing he first becomes self-centered, and later, by way of the inflation of his ego, he may become deranged as well. It has been rightly said that those who seek the great union should desire only to obey heaven and to serve humanity. All other motives are unworthy and hazardous in the extreme.

It will be apparent from the foregoing that the principal purpose of taking the Fool's Pilgrimage is to achieve a transformation within the traveler by which his self-will is voluntarily diminished in order that the universal will may increasingly reveal itself and its purposes through the human personality. The Gnostics of the first Christian centuries likened the world to a roadside tavern wherein travelers in a drunken revel forget the nature of their journey and their destination. The stupefying intoxicant administered to the wayfarer in this inn of the human condition is the willfulness and self-involvement of the human ego. Only by lessening the authority of the personal self by way of a directed, gradual discipline of internal realization can we be assured of not being deflected from our journey by the temptations along the way. The Exodus myth, referred to previously, dramatically demonstrates the conflicts that arise as the result of the opposition put forth against the journey by the personal self. How often does the traveler, limited in his outlook by the memories of the spiritually useless satisfactions of the ego, disdain the manna, or heavenly food, provided by his indwelling guiding genius? He cries out in nostalgia for the earthly food of selfishness, which had to be left behind in the course of the journey: "Who shall give us flesh to eat? We remember the fish, which we did eat in Egypt freely.... But now our soul *is* dried away; *there is* nothing at all, beside this manna, *before* our eyes." (Num. 11:4–6) Such protestations of the lesser man, however, avail little against the determined leadership and guidance of the Higher Self that, like Moses of old, lifts up its magic rod of the spiritual will and, stretching it out over the sea of obstacles, divides the waters and affords us passage.

The process of climbing the Tree of Life by way of the paths, as dramatized in the meditations on the Tarot Trumps, is Replete with difficulties, obstacles, and temptations of the above noted kind. The lore of the Kabbalah contains references to the possibility that the soul, while ascending the Tree, might fall, or slip, and thus be forced to assume once more the old position, where it was unable to hold its own during the previous attempt. Even more dire hazards are alluded to whenever the Kabbalah mentions the dark mystery of the Abyss, which is represented as a psychic gulf, separating the supernal triad of the uppermost three sephiroth, with their interconnecting paths, from the lower areas of the Tree. The soul, lacking in willingness to let go of its egoism, may be found wanting in the qualifications for entering the Divine World and, losing its equilibrium, plunge into the Abyss, there to become an unbalanced force isolated from God and humanity. This terrifying possibility is not to be regarded as a Kabbalistic disguise for the hellfire and damnation doctrines of unenlightened religiosity; but as a proper and reasonable warning that if we wish to travel on the Royal Road, we might be courting disaster if we do not remain obedient to the rules thereon. All destructive concepts, convictions, and habits, all psychological forces that engender cynicism, arrogance, and self-centeredness, lock the individual in a self-created dungeon and place him "beyond the pale" of the great scheme that works for his and all others' enlightenment.

When we attempt to achieve affinity with the great plan of the Tree of Life and its laws, which include the law of our ability to return to our essential nature, we must learn to be grateful for the spiritual opportunities available to us. We must also learn obedience to the inner command of selflessness, for to disobey this law is to break the pattern of the Tree of Life, which means to break faith with our true self. The more we perceive with our intuition the presence of the great beneficent forces in the Tree, and the more we become a part and expression of those forces, the more likely it will be that we shall develop a strong sense of appreciation, which in turn will recommend an attitude of obedience and acceptance. As we become convinced that the forces of life, of which the sephirotal Tree is the embodiment, ever support us from below and sustain us from above, we shall increasingly rid ourselves of all traces of anxious striving and strenuous haste. To hasten is to fail, for haste bears witness to the unholy pressure of ambition, which is the expression of the unregenerate ego. The traveler might well take to heart the Latin motto *Festina lente*, "Hasten slowly," along with the equally appropriate Chinese adage, "There is no hurry; heaven will wait."

Those who, throughout the ages, have undertaken to travel the many paths that together constitute the Fool's Pilgrimage have never desired to escape from incarnate existence and its responsibilities. We have spoken, throughout the earlier chapters, of the psychological distinctions existing between the basic tendencies of Eastern and Western religious philosophies. Eastern mystics seek to approach reality by retiring into themselves, while their Western counterparts are more inclined to direct their inner resources toward the world. When viewed in a proper perspective, this difference does not appear as a conflict, but rather as an emphasis, rooted in the fact that the Occidental is predominantly an extrovert and the Oriental, an introvert. Whether God be experienced as the innermost or as the furthermost, it follows that this experience must be made to bear on our present lives on earth. The philosophy of the Kabbalah affirms the human need for a deep, abiding contact with the eternal causes and powers from which our existence is suspended. At the same time, it also instructs us to return from the supernal regions to the world and live outwardly what we have realized internally, proving that we can remain uncontaminated by the pressures of environment. The aforementioned phrase, "Kether is in Malkuth," can also be understood to mean that we ourselves must make manifest the presence of the Supernal Source within the kingdom of earthly existence by way of our own willingness to demonstrate divinity within the framework of our humanity.

The noted Jewish scholar, A. J. Heschel, is credited with the saying that Ezekiel was so overwhelmed by the glory of God that he fell on his face, but it was only when he stood up that the Word came to him. Ezekiel is frequently regarded as the very embodiment of the profundities of mysticism that gave rise to the Kabbalah as we know it today. More than anything else, the Kabbalah represents a system of creative linkage between spirit and flesh, between subjective experience and objective deed. In the meditations on the paths of the Tree of Life, we have attempted to suggest to the reader the mechanism of this creative linkage. In the accompanying chapters, we have endeavored to present for consideration the quintessence of the information relevant to the understanding and practice of the joining of spirit and flesh. The forging of this creative link is not a one-time task; rather, it could be said to continue from year to year and perhaps from lifetime to lifetime, throughout eternity. Endless is the search for truth, the quest for the Divine. As J. R. R. Tolkien expressed it in his charming symbolic fantasy, *The Lord of the Rings*:

> The Road goes ever on, and on,
> Down from the door where it began.

Now far away the road has gone,
And I must follow, if I can.
Pursuing it with weary feet
Until it joins some larger way
Where many paths and errands meet,
And whither then, I cannot say.

It is not given to us to see the end of the Royal Road. From the earthly kingdom it leads, with many twists and turns, to the heavenly city; and from there it returns to the sphere of the elements, the arena of living, once more. This road needs no eulogy, requires no justification. It defies rational analysis, as it does philosophical speculation. It is the highway of the King, connecting the splendid cities of the immortal empire of authentic being. Its only real significance to us is its never-failing usefulness. By study, thought, aspiration, and meditation, by prayer, ritual, and dedicated living, we can travel this road, and for our labors we receive rewards beyond measure. If we keep the laws of the Fool's Pilgrimage, these laws in turn will keep us. Through the experience of the marvelous structure of the imperishable pattern, we shall come first to respect, then to admire, and ultimately to adore in dedicated rapture the great Totality within which we exist, and which is the beginning and the ending of the road, as well as the road itself. And if, in the fullness of time, at the conclusion of some unnumbered aeonian cycle of journeys we should be gathered to our fathers, we shall then find our place by the waters of life in the orchard of immortality.

# APPENDIX

## *Astral Travel: The Active Imagination*

For the sake of completeness, it may be useful to include, for the reader's consideration, a brief account of a method of progressing upward along the paths of the Tree of Life, which is in many ways related to the much simpler one to which the foregoing manual is devoted. We are referring to the method of traveling on the paths astrally, or by way of what has been called "astral clairvoyance" and more anciently "skrying in the spirit vision." In modern psychology, such terms as "directed reverie" and the exercise of "active imagination" might be considered to be the equivalents of the former expressions. The word *astral* means "starry," or "star like," and by it is meant a plane of consciousness, or an area of imaginative experience, which possesses the quality of a shimmering, pulsating luminosity, similar to the luminous appearance of the celestial bodies on the starry night sky. Occultists usually distinguish between an "astral plane" and an "astral body," the latter being a counterpart of the physical body of man, but composed of the substance of the astral plane and thus serving as the vehicle of the travel of consciousness within the dimension of the astral plane.

How far these concepts should be taken literally, or to what extent they may represent a particular attempt to symbolize descriptively a variety of psychological experiences, is not our intention to determine. What is important for our purpose is to know that such experiences exist and that to some people they occur spontaneously, while in most others they can be induced through the use of the creative imagination stimulated by various exercises.

The Hermetic Order of the Golden Dawn—an esoteric organization founded in England in the latter part of the nineteenth century that became practically nonexistent by the middle of the twentieth—had a great practical interest in the Tree of Life, which it used as the basis for its system of consciousness expansion. As mentioned earlier, this organization was also responsible for the widespread interest in the use of the Tarot Arcana as symbolic of the paths and for the particular order of attributing the Arcana to the paths, which we have followed in our foregoing treatise. The Order presented its members with a graded system of instruction and ritual practice, upon the completion of certain portions of which the member attained to the status of a certain degree or grade. These grades were organized on the pattern of the Tree of Life, the lowest grade corresponding to Malkuth, the Kingdom, and the highest to Kether, the Crown. The names of the degrees were as follows:

Malkuth — Zelator
Geburah — Adeptus Major
Yesod — Theoricus
Chesed — Adeptus Exemptus
Hod — Practicus
Binah — Magister Templi
Netzach — Philosophus
Chokmah — Magus
Tiphareth — Adeptus Minor
Kether — Ipissimus

It must be kept in mind (as, regrettably, some members of the Order neglected to do) that a grade system of this nature can at best but symbolize the identified levels of attainment in the course of inner progress; going through the outer ritual of the conferring of a certain grade by no means indicates that the aspirant has actually reached the corresponding level of consciousness.

In addition to the correlation of the grades with the sephiroth, the ability to travel on the paths astrally represented another important way in which the Order made the Tree of Life a part of the magical work of its members. Such astral path working, or traveling, was usually undertaken from a lower sephirah to a higher one, or from left to right on the paths that cross the Tree laterally.

The first task consisted in formulating in the inner vision the picture of a temple, which represented the sephirah, in which the path began. Certain distinctive features were assigned to each such temple, so that it would carry the general symbolism of the sephirah it was designed to represent. The temple was always to contain a central altar with a light burning upon it and two pillars, one dark and the other light in color, representative of the pillar of severity and the pillar of mercy on the Tree of Life. Out of the temple, through a gateway, one entered the path leading to the next sephirah. The gateway faced in the direction required by the path, and across it there was to appear on a veil or curtain the image of the appropriate Tarot Trump. The astral traveler was advised to make an invocation to the sephirah from which he began, which was expressed in the person's own words, but which included the God Name attributed to the sephirah and the name of the archangel associated with it. The traveler was then ready to begin the astral trip on the path.

The first step involved approaching the Tarot Trump at the gate and, through the exercise of the magical imagination, walking into its scenery and beyond. The Tarot Arcanum obviously must have taken on a three-dimensional astral form for this purpose. In addition to the Arcanum, which represents the starting point, as it were, there were three additional marks of recognition that might enable a traveler to make certain of the path on which he found himself. The first encountered, after leaving the scenery of the Tarot Trump behind, would be the appropriate Hebrew letter to be found at the midpoint of the path, composed either of white light or of the appropriate color of the path. At the far end of the path could be found the appropriate astrological sign, and beyond it could be perceived the outside of the temple of the next sephirah, which represented the termination of the path. It being not considered advisable to enter the temple of the next sephirah unless one intended to progress to another path, one was then advised to retrace one's steps and return to the original temple. The imagined journey was closed with an offering of grateful thanks to the God Name and the Archangel of the Sephirah, after which the traveler would return to ordinary physical consciousness once more. The operation of concluding the journey was considered to be of crucial importance, and no lingering within the area of astral consciousness was permitted after the completion of the journey.

Authorities conversant with the original techniques of the Hermetic Order of the Golden Dawn assert that, in astral path work such as the foregoing paragraphs describe, the traveler would frequently meet spontaneous images that did not form a part of the standard scenery of the path, as it were. Such spontaneous images always have some bearing on the personal relationship of the traveler to the path upon which he encounters them, and therefore, they should be meditated upon subsequently in order to receive the full benefit from their manifestation. Members of the Order were taught a system of checking to ascertain whether or not a spontaneously arising image was genuine. The appropriate Hebrew letter or astrological symbol would be projected mentally by the traveler upon the image, and if it did not dissolve the picture it was regarded as genuine.

As might be deduced from the foregoing, the technique of traveling the paths astrally could be regarded as but a slightly more glamorous version of the system of guided meditation suggested in our present treatise. The qualitative difference between meditation and astral visualization is not as great as some might make it out to be. Some people have a more active magical imagination than others and are prone to perceive the spiritual qualities of the paths visually. Whether the realizations arising out of the meditative process tend to become visual, or whether they assume a less glamorous aspect, is not of great importance. What matters is that the individual personality be enabled to establish communication with the various spiritual qualities of the paths and thus assimilate into mundane consciousness the mysteries of the deeper, greater, and wiser world from which all living souls have come and to which they all must return.

# QUEST BOOKS

are published by
The Theosophical Society in America
Wheaton, Illinois 60189-0270,
a worldwide, nonprofit membership organization
that promotes fellowship among all peoples of the world,
encourages the study of religion, philosophy, and science,
and supports spiritual growth and healing.

Today humanity is on the verge of becoming, for the first time in its history, a global community. The only question is what kind of community it will be. Quest Books strives to fulfill the purpose of the Theosophical Society to act as a leavening; to introduce into humanity a large-mindedness, a freedom from bias, an understanding of the values of the East and West; and to point the way to human development as a means of service, both for the individual and for the whole of humankind.

For more information about Quest Books,
visit **www.questbooks.net**
For more information about the Theosophical Society,
visit **www.theosophical.org,**
or contact **Olcott@theosmail.net,**
or (630) 668-1571.

*The Theosophical Publishing House is aided by
the generous support of the KERN FOUNDATION,
a trust dedicated to Theosophical education.*